ETHICS

TOP TEN RULES
FOR PARALEGALS

ETHICS

TOP TEN RULES
FOR PARALEGALS

Deborah K. Orlik, Esq

Upper Saddle River, New Jersey 07458

Library of Congress Cataloging-in-Publication Data

Orlik, Deborah K.
  Ethics : top ten rules for paralegals / Deborah K. Orlik.—1st ed.
    p. cm.
  Includes index.
  ISBN 0-13-119321-X
  1. Legal ethics—United States. 2. Legal assistants—United States—Handbooks, manuals,
    etc. I. Title.
  KF306.Z9.O75 2006
  174'.3'0973—dc22

                                                 2005003722

Director of Production and Manufacturing: Bruce Johnson
Senior Acquisitions Editor: Gary Bauer
Editorial Assistant: Jacqueline Knapke
Marketing Manager: Leigh Ann Sims
Managing Editor—Production: Mary Carnis
Manufacturing Buyer: Ilene Sanford
Production Liaison: Denise Brown
Production Editor: Heather Willison/Carlisle Publishers Services
Composition: Carlisle Communications, Ltd.
Senior Design Coordinator: Christopher Weigand
Cover Design: Kevin Kall
Cover Image: John Labbe/Image Bank/Getty Images, Inc.
Cover Printer: Phoenix Color
Printer/Binder: RR Donnelley & Sons

The information provided in this text is not intended as legal advice for specific situations, but is meant solely for educational and informational purposes. Readers should retain and seek the advice of their own legal counsel in handling specific legal matters.

Pearson Education Ltd.
Pearson Education Singapore Pte. Ltd.
Pearson Education Canada Ltd.
Pearson Education—Japan
Pearson Education Australia Pty. Limited

Pearson Education North Asia Ltd.
Pearson Educación de Mexico, S. A. de C.V.
Pearson Education Malaysia Pte. Ltd.
Pearson Education, Upper Saddle River, New Jersey

10 9 8 7 6 5 4 3 2 1
ISBN 0-13-119321-X

To my father. I miss him every day.

Pearson Legal Series

Pearson Legal Series provides paralegal/legal studies to students and educators with the publishing industry's finest content and best service. We offer an extensive selection of products for over 70 titles and we continue to grow with more new titles each year. We also provide:

- online resources for instructors and students
- state-specific materials
- custom publishing options from Pearson Custom Publishing group

To locate your local Pearson Prentice Hall representative, visit *www.prenhall.com.*

To view Pearson Legal Series titles and to discover a wide array of resources for both instructors and students, please visit our website at

www.prenhall.com/legal_studies

Pearson
Prentice Hall
Legal Series

CONTENTS

RULE 5   MAKE LEGAL SERVICES AVAILABLE   61

RULE 6   REPRESENT EACH CLIENT WITH ZEAL AND DEDICATION . . . WITHIN THE BOUNDS OF THE LAW   71

RULE 7 DON'T PRACTICE LAW
WITHOUT A LICENSE   89

PREFACE

This is my 5th, no, 6th attempt to write a textbook that is interesting, engaging, and, dare I say it, fun to read. To me, there is little more fascinating than a convoluted ethical issue. You're thinking: get a life. Perhaps . . . but, ask any teacher: ethics is one of the best subjects to teach, primarily because there are so many "right" answers. I think it is fun to learn for the same reason.

Although our study of "ethics" is the study of rules of law and not the study of "morals," be prepared to use your own morality, your own thresholds of right and wrong, to discuss the scenarios in this book. This is a good thing because it is your morality that you take with you into the workplace. This course of study will give you an opportunity to take out some feelings and opinions you may not have used in a while, dust them off, and get them ready to go to work.

No one book can provide the answers to all ethical issues. But this text will give you a starting place. By the end of your course of study, you should be able to (1) identify an ethical issue (2) put it into a general category—one of the Top Ten Rules; and (3) know where to start researching the answer to your particular issue.

Your goal, then, is to engrave these ten rules of ethics on your arm, or somewhere else where you won't lose or forget them. My goal is to make that something you really want to do. The goal of the paralegal profession is this: protect the public.

Don't forget that in addition to this textbook, there are materials on the publisher's website that will assist you in your study of professional responsibility. Those materials can be found here: *www.prenhall.com/orlik*.

Before you begin, go get a copy of your state's rules of professional conduct that you can keep and annotate. You can study the ABA Model Rules or Model Codes all you want, but in the final analysis, those models are not the law. They are only models, examples that your state used when it created and codified its own rules of professional responsibility (except, of course, unless you're in California where neither of those models applies). Get a copy of your state's rules of professional conduct for lawyers, including any evidence code sections that apply, and get all of that itty-bitty print enlarged. Create a notebook where you can divide your state's codes into the categories of your Top Ten Rules. Now you're ready. Good luck.

Special thanks to the reviewers of this text: Bob Diotalevi, Florida Gulf Coast University, Fort Meyers, FL; Denise Hill, College of St. Mary, Omaha NE; Taylor Morton, Legal Education Consultant, Altadena, CA; Annalinda Ragazzo, Bryant and Stratton College, Rochester, NY.

INTRODUCTION

Why do we have to study ethics? Hmmmm . . . good question. The first reason is that it is a required course. In order to be accredited by various institutions, your paralegal education must include the study of ethics. The second reason is although it may seem like an intuitive subject, the study of legal ethics is not the same as the study of ethics that you might find in a philosophy program. The study of legal ethics is the study of rules of law. These are rules of law that you must know to be a successful paralegal. You must know them because others around you may not know them. You must know them for day-to-day survival in your new profession. And, you might find that learning them is kind of fun and leads to all sorts of interesting and exciting discussions.

Legal ethics is also known as "professional responsibility." Lawyers have been writing laws about professional responsibility—about their responsibilities to the judicial system, to the public, and to each other—for over a century. Luckily, we don't have to study the really old laws.

Our study necessarily includes the American Bar Association (ABA). The ABA is a voluntary organization of lawyers. You should take a look at its Web site—*www.abanet.org*—to see all of the things that it does. For our purposes, however, the ABA does two things: (1) It has written a document for lawyers regarding the proper use of paralegals, and (2) It has provided model laws dealing with professional responsibility applicable to both lawyers and paralegals.

The way this drafting works is this: some members of the ABA who are knowledgeable in any particular subject get together and draft some sample laws, called Codes or Rules, and then they provide these samples (models) to the state legislatures for their consideration. This saves the states from having to spend the resources to draft their own rules and it provides for some continuity in the rules from state to state. They do this in all sorts of subjects, but we're only concerned about the ones they have written about legal ethics.

The ABA produced its first Rules of professional responsibility in 1908. We won't bother with them. The second group of Rules it drafted is called the Model Code of Professional Responsibility. The Model Code had nine *canons* and each canon had a set of Ethical Considerations and Disciplinary Rules. You will see them referred to in the text as ECs and DRs. The ECs are aspirational. They set forth the reasons for the canons and contain

You probably want to see the ABA publication called *Model Guidelines for the Utilization of Legal Assistant Services*. It was last revised in February 2004. You can see it in pdf format on the ABA's Web site, *www.abanet.org*.

A *canon* is an accepted rule or principle or a set of standards.

guidelines that you may want to consider when making ethical choices. The DRs are exactly that. If a DR is violated, discipline by the appropriate authority is likely. The Model Code was written in the 1960s, and a few states still have rules of professional conduct that are modeled after this format: the Canon, Ethical Consideration, and Disciplinary Rule.

In the 1980s, the ABA wrote a revised model. This one is called the Model Rules of Professional Conduct. The format of this model is entirely different. The idea of the canons was abandoned. The Rule is stated in the form of an ordinary rule and then Comments are provided that help you interpret and use the Rule in context. The Rule may be subject to many interpretations, but the Comments help to narrow them down.

Almost all states have adopted the new format and most of the text of the Rules model. A few states are still using laws based on the Code model. California, ever the individual, never adopted either format.

Although you will see the Models referred to in many writings, it is not the ABA's Model that has the force of law. *Only the rules actually adopted by your state have the force of law in your state.* You probably don't want to quote a Model Rule in your work. You always want to refer to your own state codes. If this looks a little confusing right now, don't worry. There are many examples in the text you are about to read that will help clarify this stuff.

The ABA has released some amendments to the Model Rules—called the 2000 Rules—because they were supposed to have been available in the year 2000. Your state may be in the process of amending its rules of professional responsibility to adopt some of the changes suggested by the ABA in this last group of amendments, so you should be on the lookout for changes in this law.

Finding the law on ethics isn't always easy, but if you walk step by step through the Top Ten Rules and do the Internet and library exercises suggested, by the time you've reached Rule #10, you'll have all of the research tricks down cold.

HAVE INTEGRITY

WHY START HERE?

If you're wondering why Rule #1 is "have integrity," the answer is this: if we don't have integrity, the rest of the rules are useless. Integrity means steadfast adherence to an ethical code, and that's what you will be asked to do when you enter the legal profession. All of the Top Ten Rules require steadfast adherence. That's the beginning. Rule #1 includes our duty (if we actually have one) to report our own misconduct and the misconduct of others, prohibitions on intimate relationships with clients and why these relationships are prohibited, the pervasive problems stemming from drug and alcohol abuse, and sexual harassment in the workplace. If all of these topics seem dark or depressing to you, here's the good news: for the most part, legal professionals are good people. They enter the field of law, just as you are, out of a desire to help people—to help the public. The topics we discuss in Rule #1 are things that you must know so that you can recognize the issue if it comes up and so that you know how to deal with it. That's the other good news: after reading about Rule #1, you'll be prepared to face these issues in the (we hope) rare instance that they occur.

WE'RE IN CHARGE OF OUR OWN PROFESSION

United States Supreme Court Chief Justice Cardozo, as early as 1928, recognized that every person who works in the legal profession has a duty to police the profession for traces of impropriety. In *People ex rel. Karlin v. Culkin*,[1] he wrote: "If the house is to be cleaned, it is for those who occupy and govern it, rather than for strangers, to do the noisome work." What he meant was this: if the legal profession does not want to be judged by lay people, it will have to police itself. He also wrote that if the legal profession maintains a high standard, it will not be vulnerable to outside criticism.

Report Violations—The Lawyer's Duty

We are talking about the ABA Model Codes and Model Rules here. If you don't remember what they are, go back to the Introduction on page xiii and review.

Model Code EC 1-4 and Model Rule 8.3 require lawyers to report violations of the Disciplinary Rules to the Bar in order to maintain the integrity of the profession. This is what Chief Justice Cardozo was talking about and it is called *self-policing*.

"Should" is discretionary.

> **EC 1-4** The integrity of the profession can be maintained only if conduct of lawyers in violation of the Disciplinary Rules is brought to the attention of the proper officials. A lawyer should reveal voluntarily to those officials all unprivileged knowledge of conduct of lawyers which he believes clearly to be in violation of the Disciplinary Rules.

"Shall" is mandatory.

> **Rule 8.3(a)** A lawyer having knowledge that another lawyer has committed a violation of the rules of professional conduct that raises a substantial question as to that lawyer's honesty, trustworthiness or fitness as a lawyer in other respects, shall inform the appropriate professional authority.

Report Violations—The Paralegal's Duty

Bearing in mind that the ethical codes of the paralegal associations do not carry the weight of law (are not enforceable), here is what they say: National Federation of Paralegal Association's Model Code includes two ethical considerations that require reporting misconduct. EC 1-2(f) requires the advising of the proper authority of any trust fund violations, and EC 1-3(d) requires reporting any action that demonstrates fraud, deceit, or dishonesty.

These reporting rules are typically called "Fink Rules."[2] They all exclude reporting any information that is confidential (a concept we tackle in Rule #2), but they otherwise require you to give the information to a *tribunal* that asks for it. The Model Rule and NFPA Model Code, however, go even further than requiring disclosure when asked. They require you to report professional misconduct even when there is no inquiry. Again, however, these are just "model" rules. They don't have the force of law. What you want to know is what your state law says. Let's take some examples.

Tribunal means a court of justice.

> The Lawyer's Code of Professional Responsibility—
> New York State (2002 edition)
>
> *EC 1-4*

We use New York as an example here because New York's code is modeled after the ABA Model Codes.

> The integrity of the profession can be maintained only if conduct of lawyers in violation of the Disciplinary Rules is brought to the attention of the proper officials. A lawyer should reveal voluntarily to those officials all knowledge, other than knowledge protected as a confidence or secret, of conduct of another lawyer which the lawyer believes clearly to be a violation of the Disciplinary Rules that raises

a substantial question as to the other lawyer's honesty, trustworthiness or fitness in other respects as a lawyer. A lawyer should, upon request, serve on and assist committees and boards having responsibility for the administration of the Disciplinary Rules.

So, if you're in New York, and if we subscribe to the belief that paralegals and lawyers are to be guided by the same rules of professional conduct (which I hope we are by now), you "should" (your choice) tell "the proper officials" (whoever they may be depending on the situation) about the conduct of a lawyer or paralegal <u>if</u> that conduct is a violation of the other rules of professional conduct <u>and</u> the conduct leads you to believe that the lawyer or paralegal is not honest or trustworthy or otherwise is not fit for duty.

WHAT DO YOU THINK?

What is an example of this kind of conduct? If you saw the file clerk stealing a wallet from a co-worker's office, would you report it? Would you still report this theft if the thief was your supervising attorney? Why? Why not? Instead of reporting this conduct, would you confront the wrongdoing file clerk? How about the wrongdoing attorney?

Let's take another example:

Texas Disciplinary Rules of Professional Conduct

Rule 8.03 Reporting Professional Misconduct

(a) Except as permitted in paragraphs (c) or (d), a lawyer having knowledge that another lawyer has committed a violation of applicable rules of professional conduct that raises a substantial question as to that lawyer's honesty, trustworthiness or fitness as a lawyer in other respects, <u>shall inform</u> the appropriate disciplinary authority.

> We use Texas as an example here because its code is modeled after the ABA Model Rules.

(b) Except as permitted in paragraphs (c) or (d), a lawyer having knowledge that a judge has committed a violation of applicable rules of judicial conduct that raises a substantial question as to the judge's fitness for office <u>shall inform</u> the appropriate authority.

(c) A lawyer having knowledge or suspecting that another lawyer or judge whose conduct the lawyer is required to report pursuant to paragraphs (a) or (b) of this Rule is impaired by chemical dependency on alcohol or drugs or by mental illness <u>may report</u> that person to an approved peer assistance program rather than to an appropriate disciplinary authority. If a lawyer elects that option, the lawyer's report to the approved peer assistance program shall disclose any disciplinary violations that the reporting lawyer would otherwise have to disclose to the authorities referred to in paragraphs (a) and (b).

> Note that this code makes some reporting mandatory. It says "shall inform" in the first two sections but makes reporting drug/alcohol abuse discretionary.

(d) This rule does not require disclosure of knowledge or information otherwise protected as confidential information.

> And here's the part where confidential information is excluded.

Let's take one more example:

Kansas Judicial Branch
Rules Adopted by the Supreme Court
Discipline of Attorneys
Rule 8.3 Reporting Professional Misconduct

Kansas also used ABA Model Rule 8.3 but amended it in a different way.

(a) A lawyer having knowledge of any action, inaction, or conduct which in his or her opinion constitutes misconduct of an attorney under these rules <u>shall inform</u> the appropriate professional authority.

(b) A lawyer having knowledge that a judge has committed a violation of applicable rules of judicial conduct that raises a substantial question as to the judge's fitness for office shall inform the appropriate authority.

Where this rule refers to Rule 1.6, that's the Kansas rule on confidential information.

(c) This rule does not require disclosure of information otherwise protected by Rule 1.6. In addition, a lawyer is not required to disclose information concerning any such violation which is discovered through participation in a Substance Abuse Committee, Service to the Bar Committee or similar committee sponsored by a state or local bar association, or by participation in a self-help organization such as Alcoholics Anonymous, through which aid is rendered to another lawyer who may be impaired in the practice of law.

How Does This Apply to Me?

There is some authority for the proposition that if the lawyer does not report the ethical violations of opposing counsel, that misconduct cannot later be used as the basis for an appeal.[3] So, for example, if you have knowledge that opposing counsel is tampering with the jury or trying to influence them in some illegal way, and you don't tell your supervising attorney so that the misconduct can be brought to the attention of the judge, you can't wait for the trial to be over and then, presuming you have lost, use that jury tampering charge to ask for a new trial or an appeal.

> **WHAT DO YOU THINK?**
> Is there a flaw in that argument? What would be the likely outcome in your state?

If you don't know what privileged information is, you have to read Rule #2.

Does the legal professional have to report his/her own dishonest act? Some commentators say no. Here's their logic: (1) Privileged information is protected from mandatory disclosure; (2) Your own criminal conduct is protected by the Fifth Amendment privilege against self-incrimination, and so you don't have to report yourself. Model Rule 8.3, you should note,

> One of the very few cases where an attorney was actually disciplined for not ratting-out a lawyer who did something unethical is *In re Himmel,* 533 N.E.2d 790 (Ill. 1988). Here are the facts: Attorney Himmel represented a woman who claimed that another attorney (Casey) had taken off with her money. Himmel agreed to get the money back from Casey in exchange for one-third of the recovery. Casey agreed to settle the case. The settlement agreement that Himmel drafted included the woman's agreement not to initiate any criminal, civil, or disciplinary action against Casey. Himmel was later disciplined for failing to notify the appropriate authorities of Casey's misappropriation of the client's money. The disciplining authority found that Himmel possessed **unprivileged information** of another attorney's misconduct. Himmel's argument that he did not report Casey because his client directed him not to do so was an unacceptable excuse. The opinion pointed out that Himmel's primary duty is to **protect the public** and **assist in maintaining the integrity of the legal profession.** The lawyer cannot get around the rules by saying that he or she was instructed not to tell.
> The *Himmel* decision has been cited as authority in other Illinois cases standing for the proposition that the attorney's duty to report is "absolute."

says that the legal professional with knowledge "of <u>another</u> [legal professional]" must report. In theory, that excludes self-reporting.[4]

California has no duty to report another person but does require self-reporting under Business & Professions Code § 6068. There also does not appear to be an equivalent under the NALA Code of Ethics; however, that Code does require "the legal assistant to avoid conduct which would cause the lawyer to be unethical or even appear to be unethical, and loyalty to the employer is incumbent upon the legal assistant."[5]

Does This Really Apply to the Paralegal?

It has been theorized that, because nonlawyers such as law clerks and paralegals are governed by their states' rules governing lawyer professional responsibility, we have an affirmative duty to report unethical practices of an attorney or another legal professional. NFPA Model Code EC 1-2(f) makes reporting an affirmative duty in the case of dishonesty pertaining to client trust accounts or other client assets. NFPA Model Code EC 1-3(d) makes reporting fraud an affirmative duty regardless of the object of the fraud or who will be hurt. **However, there is no statutory or case authority that specifically extends this duty to any nonlawyer legal professional. It is all academic—something we talk about, but not necessarily something that is required by law.**

As we saw in our examples above, Rule 8.3 is one of the rules in the ABA Model Rules that was left out or amended by some states as they were adopting the Model as their own. Some states made reporting certain situations mandatory. You need to research the authority in your state and consider reporting that behavior to the "proper authorities." Case law indicates that the person who reports pursuant to 8.3 is immune from a later lawsuit for slander, libel, and malicious prosecution[6] but may not necessarily use reporting misconduct to prove retaliatory discharge.[7]

The Threat of Disciplinary Action

It is improper to use the threat of disciplinary action to gain an advantage in a case.[8] It is okay to explain to the client how to go about filing a disciplinary complaint, but not to encourage the filing of a disciplinary complaint as a tactic in winning. Further, the lawyer "must" (it's mandatory) withdraw from the representation if the client insists on using such a threat.

Who Are the Proper Authorities?

Once the decision is made to report, to whom should the report be made? Who is the "proper authority"? Well, there is no definitive answer to that question. Within a firm or corporation, the proper authority may be found inside the company. Perhaps there is a managing partner, office manager, or ethics committee in charge of allegations of improper conduct. If not, the state bar, district attorney, or attorney general may be the proper authority depending upon the severity of the wrongdoing and who the wrongdoer is.

If asked by a proper tribunal, the paralegal must always tell the truth about personal knowledge of the unethical practices of another legal professional. Bear in mind that the tribunal probably has the right to call a paralegal or other law firm employee as a witness in any ethics action before it or before a court. Responding truthfully to questions from a law enforcement agency is mandatory, assuming the information is not protected by some evidentiary privilege or rule of confidentiality.

There is no authority that reporting unethical conduct is mandatory for you as a paralegal. There will be times, however, when you feel that reporting someone else's conduct is the right thing to do. When making a determination about reporting unethical or criminal behavior of another legal professional, consider the following (not exclusive) factors:

1. Do you have all of the facts?
2. Who is being harmed by the behavior? The public?
3. What are your motives for reporting the behavior?
4. Who is the "proper authority" in your law firm?

A case from Pennsylvania (Brown v. Hammond (E.D.Pa 1993) 810 F.Supp. 644) suggests that the client is definitely not the proper authority for purposes of reporting misconduct. In that case, the paralegal had evidence of "fraudulent overbilling" of a client. The paralegal told the client about the billing fraud and was fired from her job for "blowing the whistle." In the paralegal's wrongful termination action against the employer, the Pennsylvania court said that the paralegal should not have made "gratuitous disclosures" of the alleged misconduct to the affected clients. The court mentioned that there were "proper authorities" and "persons responsible for reporting such conduct or for protecting the public interest" but did not elucidate on who those authorities might be.

The Pennsylvania court also drew a distinction between having evidence of others engaging in unethical billing practices and the paralegal being asked or required to engage in similar practices. The judge wrote that "no employee should be forced to choose between his or her livelihood and engaging in fraud or other criminal conduct." In other words, the Pennsylvania employment laws would offer some protection to the employee who is discharged for refusing to personally commit fraud but will not protect the employee discharged for blowing the whistle on the employer who is committing fraud. Does your state have whistle-blower protection?

5. Who is the "proper law enforcement authority" in your state?

6. How much do you need your job? Can you risk retaliation?

7. In your state, is there an affirmative duty to report misconduct?

8. Are there laws in your state that protect "whistle-blowers"?

9. Is there someone else with whom you can discuss the problem to get another perspective? A member of the clergy, doctor, teacher?

10. Does anyone else have knowledge of the wrong behavior who could support your position?

GENERAL AND MISCELLANEOUS MISCONDUCT PROHIBITED

The ABA Model Code EC 1-5 requires us to maintain the highest standards of professional conduct and to encourage others to do so as well. It says that we are to be "temperate and dignified" and "refrain from all illegal and morally reprehensible conduct." This is because people who are engaged in the practice of law are held high in the public esteem.

If we want to know what conduct is considered professional misconduct, the ABA Model Rules more closely define the specific conduct:

Rule 8.4 Misconduct: It Is Professional Misconduct for a Lawyer to:

(a) violate or attempt to violate the Rules of Professional Conduct, knowingly assist or induce another to do so, or do so through the acts of another;

(b) commit a criminal act that reflects adversely on the lawyer's honesty, trustworthiness or fitness as a lawyer in other respects;

(c) engage in conduct involving dishonesty, fraud, deceit or misrepresentation;

(d) engage in conduct that is prejudicial to the administration of justice;

(e) state or imply an ability to influence improperly a government agency or official <u>or to achieve results by means that violate the Rules of Professional Conduct or other law</u>; or

(f) knowingly assist a judge or judicial officer in conduct that is a violation of applicable rules of judicial conduct or other law.

Mississippi adopted 8.4 verbatim in its original form, without the underlined section of (e).

North Carolina adopted (a) through (f) and added this one more subsection:
(g) intentionally prejudice or damage his or her client during the course of the professional relationship, except as may be required by Rule 3.3. (Rule 3.3 is North Carolina's rule on telling the court the truth.)

New Hampshire adopted a, b, c, the not-underlined portion of e, and f . . . but not d.

This would be a good time to look up your state's rule on "general misconduct" but the bigger question is what does this rule mean in reality?

Here is Maine's version of the General Misconduct Rule:

3.2 Admission, Disclosure and Misconduct
. . . (f) Other Misconduct. A lawyer shall not:

(1) directly or indirectly violate, circumvent, or subvert any provision of the Maine Bar Rules;

(2) engage in illegal conduct that adversely reflects on the lawyer's honesty, trustworthiness, or fitness as a lawyer in other respects;

(3) engage in conduct involving dishonesty, fraud, deceit, or misrepresentation

(4) engage in conduct that is prejudicial to the administration of justice.

Here's an example of how the general misconduct rule works: a lawyer who told the small claims court that money she owed to her landlord had been paid when the lawyer knew that there were insufficient funds in her bank account to cover the check engaged in conduct involving dishonesty, fraud, deceit, or misrepresentation as set forth in Rule 8.4.[9] This was true even though the improper conduct had to do with the lawyer's personal life as opposed to her representation of a client.

General Misconduct and the Paralegal

Case law indicates that under the doctrine of *respondeat superior,* employer-attorneys will be liable for the criminal or other dishonest acts performed by their employee-nonlawyers (including paralegals) under the "course and scope" of the employee's employment. However, it is still unclear as to whether paralegals will be held responsible if they know of the dishonest act of an attorney or another nonlawyer and do not report it to the proper authorities. The NFPA Model Code suggests that they should be. And, of course, these criminal or other dishonest acts will be cause for termination.

Respondeat superior is Latin for "let the master answer."

Remember: the dishonesty or level of wrongdoing should be viewed not from the vantage point of the attorney or legal assistant, but from the viewpoint of the public. "Protect the public" is the legal professional's foremost duty.

Sexual Relations with the Client

How did we get from "integrity" to sex? It is probably Arnie Becker's fault. Arnie Becker was a fictional character on a television show about lawyers that was popular in the 1990s. It seemed that Attorney Becker had an intimate relationship with all of his clients. After that show brought attention to this issue, many jurisdictions amended their professional responsibility rules to prohibit sexual relations between legal professional and client. These laws were enacted to compensate for the difficulty in separating the sound judgment that a competent legal professional needs to use from the emotional decisions or bias that may result from an intimate relationship between lawyer and client. Emotional detachment is essential to the ability to render competent legal services . . . or so the theory goes.

> **WHAT DO YOU THINK?**
>
> Could you be a competent legal professional (Rule #3) but stay within the bounds of the law (Rule #6) if your client was your lover?

Some states have found that an intimate relationship with a client is *per se* unethical, even when the state has no specific rule prohibiting it, because of the general public's perception that judgment will be impaired

Per se is Latin. It means "by itself" or "without more."

by such a relationship. However rational that may be, it is little comfort to those of us whose only contact with other people may be through the relationship that begins with legal representation. The rule requires that sexual relationships wait until after the legal relationship has ended.[10]

Some safe rules for dating within the legal profession were suggested in a law review article: *Comments: Dating Among the Profession: Ethical Guidance in the Area of Personal Dating Conflicts of Interest,* 34 Santa Clara Law Review 1157 (1993).

WHAT DO YOU THINK?

Should a lawyer be disbarred for having a sexual relationship with a client? What other facts do you want in order to make this decision? Take a look at: *The Florida Bar v. Senton,*— So.2d—, 29 Fla.L. Weekly S463 (Fla., No. SC00-762, 9/2/2004).

Stress and Alcohol/Drug Abuse

Let's face it. The legal profession is extremely stressful. And here's another truism: people who are stressed often turn to alcohol and/or drugs. The rules that govern us have provisions designed to protect the public from legal professionals who are physically or mentally incapable of doing their job. EC 1-6, the last ethical consideration under ABA Model Code Canon 1, requires legal professionals to police their profession for signs of mental and emotional instability. Model Rule 8.4(d) says that it is professional misconduct for a lawyer to "engage in conduct that is prejudicial to the administration of justice," rather a broad admonition by which the Bar can discipline an attorney for drug or alcohol addiction. You might want to see if your state's laws include a version of Model Rule 1.16(a)(2) that requires the lawyer to withdraw from representation when "the lawyer's physical or mental condition materially impairs the lawyer's ability to represent the client."

The ABA established the Commission on Impaired Attorneys all the way back in 1988.[11] The commission works as an informational bureau for lawyer-impairment issues and programs. The commission has published surveys of lawyer assistance programs, including each state's opinions on confidentiality and immunity rules and case law. These surveys make it clear that the states differ widely on these issues. For example, New York has held that drug addiction may be considered a mitigating factor in attorney discipline.[12] Simultaneously, another state court refused to recognize drug and alcohol addiction as a mitigating factor.[13]

In the 1990s there was a movement among legal professionals to treat alcoholism and drug dependency as diseases that need to be medically treated. Many states created diversion programs that take the lawyer off the disciplinary track and into a program for counseling, treatment, and monitoring.[14] (See *www.otherbar.org.*) The Utah State Bar Association's Web site reports surveys showing 20% of lawyers and judges suffer from alcohol dependence. Its program "Lawyers Helping Lawyers" is designed as a support mechanism for lawyers suffering from mental illness, substance abuse, or any other disabling condition. You can find out more about this program on the Utah Bar Web site: *www.utahbar.org.*

There is no doubt that drug and alcohol abuse impairs a person's ability to do competent work. The pervasiveness of the problem is staggering. A survey of managing partners of law firms based in one large U.S. city showed that 82% of the partners polled had worked with a partner with "personal problems" that affected job performance; 39% said that the "personal problem" was alcoholism.[15] In 2002, 120 million Americans 12 years old and older reported drinking within 30 days of the survey. That's 51% of our population. Fifty-four million reported binge drinking. If that didn't scare you, this should: about 1 in 7 Americans aged 12 or older in 2002 (14.2 percent, or 33.5 million persons) drove under the influence of alcohol at least once in the 12 months prior to the survey interview.

In 2002, an estimated 19.5 million Americans were current users of illicit drugs, meaning they used an illicit drug at least once during the 30 days prior to the interview.[16] That's 8.3% of our population. When we're talking about drugs here, we're not just talking about marijuana or cocaine, although marijuana is the most commonly used illicit drug. In 2002, opioid pain relievers accounted for about 10% of drug abuse-related emergency department visits. Oxycodone and hydrocodone are the most frequently abused pain relievers. Between 1994 and 2002, abuse of oxycodone increased 450% and hydrocodone abuse increased 170%. For updated statistics on all sorts of drug and alcohol related statistics, go to the Web site of the U.S. Health Department's Substance Abuse and Mental Health Services Administration: *www.samhsa.gov.*

There is also no doubt that well-meaning friends and associates make the dependent legal professional worse by "enabling."[17]

Nonlawyers who work in the highly stressful legal world are not immune from these pressures. "Paralegal burnout" is as likely to occur as attorney burnout.[18] As a paralegal, you want to be aware of the potential for abuses of drugs and alcohol among our ranks, as well as other signs of mental and emotional deterioration. Help is available if we know where to look for it. Now would be a good time to investigate the various support groups and help lines in your state or city so that you can make this information available to those who need it.

WHAT DO YOU THINK?

You are a paralegal for a sole practitioner. You are fond of your boss and want the firm to be successful both for the boss and for you. Then you discover that your boss has a serious addiction to cocaine. You have a lot of options. What would you do? What are the possible outcomes of your action or inaction?

Sexual Harassment

Why do we talk about sexual harassment here in a chapter on integrity? Because sexual harassment is another one of those uncategorized "general misconduct" behaviors. It is illegal. It is unethical, but it is also something that happens, and you ought to know what to do about it if and when you see it or if you are a victim.

Here's the law: Title VII of the Civil Rights Act of 1964 makes it "an unlawful employment practice for an employer . . . to discriminate against any individual with respect to his compensation, terms, conditions, or privileges of employment, because of such individual's race, color, religion, sex, or national origin."[19] Without question, when a supervisor harasses a subordinate because of the subordinate's sex, that supervisor discriminates on the basis of sex.[20] Sexual harassment is, among other things, "unwelcome sexual advances, requests for sexual favors, and other verbal or physical conduct of a sexual nature."[21] The victim as well as the harasser may be a woman or a man. The victim does not have to be of the opposite sex.

Here's an example: in *Weeks v. Baker & McKenzie*[22] a high-powered senior partner continually lambasted legal secretary Weeks, dropped candies in the pocket of her blouse, groped her breasts and rear end, and made sexual remarks to her and about her. When Weeks sued for sexual harassment, it became apparent that the partner's conduct was not an isolated incident but a pattern of behavior. Six other female employees who had worked for that partner came forward to testify that he had also touched them, made inappropriate remarks, and pressured them for sex. Most of the women had told the law firm management or their immediate supervisors about the sexual harassment, but the firm either ignored the complaints or simply transferred the complainants to work for other people. One woman was fired after she complained. To make matters worse, the firm concealed the partner's conduct by keeping the written complaints in the women's personnel files instead of in his. Net result: the world's largest law firm was popped for $3.5 million for failure to protect these female employees from the unlawful misconduct of a senior partner.

There's a "How to" section on the publisher's Web site just for you. Take some time now and go read "How to Deal With Supervisors" (http://www.prenhall.com/orlik).

Reporting sexual harassment is a puzzle that was exemplified on national television during Supreme Court Justice Clarence Thomas's confirmation hearings. Many people believed that the justice's accuser was trying only to make a name for herself. Many believed that she had been sexually harassed by a man who was about to become a Supreme Court justice. It takes courage and determination to make this sort of charge about a superior. For a case against a judge where the complaints of women were believed, see *Office of Disciplinary Counsel v. Campbell*[23] where a judge used his powerful position to harass inexperienced women attorneys engaged in new jobs early in their careers. The disciplining court found that the judge's unwelcome and offensive sexual remarks and physical contact were grounds for suspension in spite of his complete denial, his dozen character witnesses, and over forty reference letters lauding his exemplary life.

PROOF OF UNFIT CHARACTER

The state bar has the burden to prove an attorney's unfitness by a preponderance of the evidence. Once this charge is proven against a member of the bar, the burden of proof shifts to the guilty person to show if and when he or she is able to resume professional duties. The guilty person must show the same moral fitness as an applicant for original admission.

It is likely that paralegals will be held to the same standards and burden of proof as attorneys when paralegals are held responsible for their own actions (such as in the unauthorized practice of law). Thus far, however, it appears that in most instances it will be the employing and supervising attorneys who are held liable for the acts of their paralegals and other assistants. Misconduct in the areas covered by Rule #1 may cost paralegals their jobs, and a court could impose sanctions against them including restitution to the client. Although paralegals are not licensed by the state, the state could impose sanctions such as a temporary or permanent suspension from working as a paralegal.

RULE #1 WRAP-UP

We've finished the first Rule. How do you feel? There is some stuff in this Rule that's hard to talk about. The bad news is that there are some scary things in the practice of law. The good news is that we've covered the scariest of them. In Rule #1 we covered the concept of our duty to report our own misconduct and the misconduct of others, prohibitions on intimate relationships with clients and why they are prohibited, the pervasive problems stemming from drug and alcohol abuse, and sexual harassment in the workplace. Take a deep breath. It gets better from here.

RULE #1 REVIEW QUESTIONS

1. What is "integrity"? Why is it an important concept for study for people entering the legal profession?
2. Describe the concept of "self-policing."
3. Is there a statutory duty (a law) that says that paralegals must report the improper conduct of attorneys? or of other paralegals? What are some possible consequences of enacting such a law?
4. If you have the duty to report misconduct, what kinds of things would you have to report (mandatory), and what kinds of things should you report (discretionary)?
5. If you had absolute proof that a fellow paralegal was not working all of the hours he is reporting on his time sheets, what would you do about it, if anything?

6. If you are asked out for lunch by a client of the firm, would you go? Why or why not?

7. What are some signs that you are overly stressed from work? What are some options available to you to help remedy the problem in the short term? and long term?

8. If you witnessed a person in your firm being sexually harassed by another person, what are some of the options available to you?

9. What if you saw someone being discriminated against as a result of race or sexual preference? Is this against the law? If it is, what are some of the things you might do?

10. What is the burden of proof in a discipline case against an attorney for misconduct? How does this burden of proof compare to the burden of proof in a criminal case (proof beyond a reasonable doubt)?

---

1 162 N.E. 487 (N.Y. 1928).

2 The Fink Rule is a descendant of ABA Canon 29 that advised that the lawyer should expose corrupt or dishonest conduct in the profession.

3 See *Magness v. Magness,* 558 A.2d 807, 815 (Md.App. 1988) where the court found that the failure to report the alleged misconduct of opposing counsel was a "concession" that the alleged conduct was not a violation of any ethical standards.

4 See, *contra, Office of Disciplinary Counsel v. Casety,* 512 A.2d 607 (Pa. 1986) where the Supreme Court found that the attorney's failure to report his conviction of voluntary manslaughter immediately after his conviction was grounds for disbarment.

5 See also NALA Code of Ethics and Professional Responsibility, Canon 8.

6 See *Jarvis v. Drake,* 830 P.2d 23 (Kan. 1992).

7 See *Jacobson v. Knepper & Moga,* 185 Ill. 2d 372 (1998).

8 See Maine Ethics Op. 100 (10/4/89) opining that when the legal professional is representing someone in a malpractice case against another lawyer, it is improper to use the threat of a disciplinary complaint to gain advantage in the civil matter.

9 *Matter of Redding,* 672 N.E.2d 76 (Ind. 1996).

10 For an interesting article on this subject, see 4 Georgetown J. of Legal Ethics 1, 169 (1990).

11 The commission can be contacted at (312) 988–5359; 541 N. Fairbanks Court, Chicago, Illinois 60611.

12 *In re Winston,* 528 N.Y.S.2d 843 (1989).

13 *Twohy v. State Bar,* 769 P.2d 976 (Cal. 1989).

14 Goldberg, *Drawing the Line,* ABA Journal 32 (1990).

15 *Id.*

16 Substance Abuse and Mental Health Services Administration, *1999 National Household Survey on Drug Abuse.*

17 See *http://alcoholism.abat.com* and *http://addictiontreatment.ca* or run a search for "enabling" in any search engine.

18 *Paralegal Burnout,* 70 ABA Journal 30 (1984).

19 42 USC § 2000e - 2(a)(1).

20 *Meritor Savings Bank FSB v. Vinson,* 477 U.S. 57, 106 S.Ct. 2399 (1986); *Burlington Industries Ellerton* (1998).

21 29 CFR § 1604.11(a) (1985).

22 63 Cal. App. 4th 1128 (1998).

23 623 N.E.2d 24 (Ohio 1993).

PRESERVE THE CONFIDENCES AND SECRETS OF THE CLIENT

Most of us know that it is improper (and probably illegal) for a lawyer to divulge the secrets of a client to other people. But! Most people don't know the strange and interesting ways this rule is broken. In fact, most lawyers, even well-educated, experienced lawyers, do not fully understand this rule or the differences between the confidentiality rule and evidentiary privileges. This chapter is designed to provide some clear explanations of confidentiality and privilege and how the two are different. The possession of confidential information leads to conflicts of interest, but we discuss conflicts in Rule #8 on loyalty.

KEEP THE CLIENT'S SECRETS

The first thing we have to know is that confidentiality is a "duty." It is a "must do." The duty of confidentiality is made of two separate but dependent concepts: (1) the clients' need to feel secure that the information they give their attorneys (and everyone in the law firm) will remain confidential, based on (2) the attorneys' need to have all relevant information from the clients and the clients' need to seek early legal assistance.[1]

Think about this for a moment. If you were asked to defend a man in a criminal matter, to do your job competently, you need to know all of the facts. You need to know ALL of the facts, even the ones that seem insignificant and perhaps especially the incriminating ones. But your client is afraid to tell you the facts. Your client is afraid that you will use the facts against him, or that if you know all of the facts, you won't want to defend him, or that you will tell the authorities or other people his secrets. So, you tell your client: "It's alright. I'll keep your secrets confidential." But what does that mean exactly?

What Is "Confidential"?

It is commonly said that it is improper to divulge "confidential information." Without knowing what information is "confidential," however, we do not know what it is we should not divulge.

Model Rule of Professional Conduct 1.6 gives us the formula for determining our definition:

> A [legal professional] shall not reveal information *relating to representation of a client* unless the client consents after consultation, except for disclosures that are impliedly authorized in order to carry out the representation, and except as stated in paragraph (b).[2]

Model Rule 1.8(b) [relating to conflicts of interest] uses the same expression: "a [legal professional] shall not use information *relating to representation of a client* to the disadvantage of the client unless the client consents after consultation."

This information that "relates to the representation" doesn't have to be information learned from the client. For example, if the client's spouse, co-worker, or friend gives you information about the client's case, that is confidential, too. Think of the situation where the friend tells you that although the client is using him as an alibi, the client was not really with him at the time of the crime. Is that information that the client would want you to divulge to anyone? No. What about other information that you find out about the client on your own by reading his documents, his notes, his diary? Yes, that's confidential, too, so long as it relates to the representation of the client. Confidential information can be any information relating to the representation without regard to the source. The confidential information relating to the representation need not be personal secrets of the client, either.

Confidential information, then, is **all information relating to the representation of a client,** regardless of the source.

WHAT DO YOU THINK?

Okay. I can't tell anyone the confidential information I have, but can I "use" that information? To start your research for an answer, see *U.S. v. O'Hagan,* 521 U.S. 642 (1997).

Let's contrast the duty of confidentiality with the attorney/client privilege because this is the concept that confuses many people.

First, the attorney/client privilege is a rule of evidence that protects the client from having his or her legal team divulge client secrets **while under oath.** An example of the use of the attorney/client privilege is this: the client has confessed to a lawyer that he did the crime, but the grand jury cannot subpoena the lawyer (or paralegal!) to testify as to what the client said. Similarly, the lawyer or paralegal cannot be called upon to testify in court about this confession. In a civil court, the opposing side, which serves an interrogatory requesting all information that the client told the lawyer, will receive only "Objection. Attorney/client privilege" as a response. This is because interrogatories are questions that must be answered under oath. Interrogatories are just like questions asked in a deposition, but they are in writing. When you are part of a legal team representing a client, the opposing side cannot take your deposition and ask questions about what you know about the case (doesn't this seem obvious?) because the attorney/client privilege protects the client from having you answer those questions.

Second, there are many differences between what is confidential and what is protected by the attorney/client privilege; for example, the attorney/client privilege does not protect information that is freely available to the public. However, the obligation to keep information confidential does encompass information that is public.

Consider this scenario: the district attorney announces to the news media that your client was found in the possession of the murder weapon. The news media reports that information and it appears in the newspaper and the 5:00 news. Your client has told you that he was found with the murder weapon. You do not violate the attorney/client privilege by repeating to your roommate that the press is reporting that your client was found with the murder weapon. You do not violate the attorney/client privilege by telling your roommate that you happen to know that your client was <u>in fact</u> found in possession of the murder weapon. This is because the attorney/client privilege only applies to situations where you are under oath. You do not violate your duty of confidentiality to tell your roommate that the press is reporting that your client was found with the murder weapon because what the press is reporting, really, has nothing to do with your client or your representation of your client. However, to tell your roommate that your client <u>was in fact</u> found with the murder weapon is a violation of your duty of confidentiality because this is information relating to the representation of your client. You gained that information through your representation of the client. It is a secret. Your client told you this information in confidence. It may seem illogical that you have to keep information confidential that is already reported in the press, but the duty of confidentiality is a duty that is personal to you. It does not matter what others are doing or saying. By accepting the representation of the client, you have given your word that you will not discuss the client's confidences. **Confidentiality is a duty you have promised to your client.** Attorney/client privilege is an evidentiary privilege.

Third, the attorney/client privilege encompasses information that the lawyer (and all of the lawyer's agents) obtains from the client only. Confidentiality encompasses all information "relating to representation of a client," regardless of its source.

Fourth, The attorney/client privilege only prevents disclosure inside the judicial process. Confidentiality prevents disclosure anywhere at any time to anyone.[3]

Read slowly. This is tough stuff.

WHAT DO YOU THINK?

You have just been given a very exciting new task having to do with a very high-profile client—a movie star! You rush home and in your excitement, you begin to tell your spouse about your exciting day. You stop. You think: "Uh oh. This is confidential information." Now what do you do?

Fifth, as we discussed in Rule #1, Model Rule 8.3 says that if you know that a lawyer has committed a violation of the Rules, you must tell, but the Rule does not require disclosure of information otherwise protected by the rules regarding confidential information (Model Rule 1.6). For example, if a lawyer is a client of your law firm and tells you the facts of the crime he has committed, this is not reportable under Rule 8.3 because it is confidential under 1.6. (It is information relating to the representation of the client.) It is not discoverable by the court (as in put the lawyer on the witness stand and ask: What did your client tell you about the crime?) because it is protected by the attorney/client privilege.

In brief, the duty of confidentiality is a duty—a responsibility. The attorney/client privilege is an evidentiary privilege—a protection against disclosure.

The concept of confidentiality is always of concern to people in the legal profession, especially because of the increasing number of freelancers and contract employees. It must also be of prime concern when changing jobs (discussed in Rule #8). The most difficult aspect of this concept, however, may be the vigilance required in ordinary conversation. You and your friend are talking about Client X as you leave the office and get into the elevator. Someone else in the elevator might know someone involved in Client X's case or X's adversary. You walk to a restaurant. Someone there overhears your conversation. You go home and innocently tell your spouse about your day, including information about X, and the next day your spouse repeats X's information to an acquaintance who, unbeknownst to you or your spouse, has some connection to X's adversary.

Any one of theses example illustrates how easy it is to violate this rule. Law firm employees as well as corporate employees should not discuss confidential information about clients with their spouses or other relatives, with friends, or with strangers. An exception to this rule may be when a legal professional is undergoing psychiatric care and feels the need to discuss a case with regard to his or her feelings about it. In this instance, although the duty of confidentiality has technically been violated, the mental health professional is also bound to keep the confidences from being revealed.

Confidentiality rules differ slightly from state to state. As with all of the rules of ethics, it is important to read and understand the authority on confidentiality in your jurisdiction.

NPFA's EC 1-5(a) says that the paralegal should familiarize himself or herself with the legal authority in his or her jurisdiction as to confidential information and abide by that authority. EC 1-5(b) says that the confidential information shall not be used to the disadvantage of the client.

The NFPA Model Code: Canon 5. A paralegal shall preserve all confidential information provided by the client or acquired from other sources before, during, and after the course of the professional relations.

The NALA Model Standards simply state that "Legal Assistants should preserve the confidences and secrets of all clients."

Rule 1.6. Confidentiality of Information.

(a) A lawyer shall not reveal a confidence or secret relating to representation of a client unless the client consents after consultation, except for disclosures that are impliedly authorized in order to carry out the representation, and except as stated in paragraph (b) or Rule 3.3(a)(2). For purposes of this rule, "confidence" means information protected by the attorney-client privilege under applicable law, and "secret" means other information gained in the professional relationship if the client has requested it be held confidential or if it is reasonably foreseeable that disclosure of the information would be embarrassing or detrimental to the client. In determining whether information relating to representation of a client is protected from disclosure under this rule, the lawyer shall resolve any uncertainty about whether such information can be revealed against revealing the information.

When Is It Okay to Disclose Confidential Information?

Quite obviously, some confidential information must be disclosed. As you can see, Model Rule 1.6 specifically exempts from the nondisclosure rules any disclosures that the client authorizes after the client has been advised about any possible adverse affects from the disclosure ("unless the client consents after consultation"). Also exempted are "disclosures that are impliedly authorized in order to carry out the representation."

> (2) to establish a claim or defense on behalf of
> the lawyer in a controversy between the lawyer
> and the client, to establish a defense to a
> criminal charge or civil claim against the lawyer
> based upon conduct in which the client was
> involved, or to respond to allegations in any
> proceeding concerning the lawyer's
> representation of the client.

This allows the disclosure of information as necessary to answer inter-rogatories or to respond to other discovery.

Even though all of the information relating to the representation of the client is confidential, the law firm may use some confidential infor-mation to defend itself against a criminal or malpractice claim by the client or to collect its fees from the client. Care should be taken not to re-veal more than is necessary to accomplish the task. Using the threat of re-lease of confidential information as a weapon against the client is prohibited.

The most interesting part of this rule is the part that exempts from confidentiality information that the legal professional may have to reveal "to prevent the client from committing a [serious] criminal act," as in your client shows up with a gun and tells you she is going to use it to kill someone. You believe that she will actually try to kill. What do you do? What she told you is technically confidential. But Model Rule 1.6(b)(1) says that you don't have to keep this knowledge secret. Various states adopted this part of the rule in different forms. Some states made reveal-ing the crime mandatory, while others leave it to the discretion of the le-gal professional. Some states limited "the crime" to a crime of death or serious bodily harm, and others enlarged it to include fraud. California only included an exemption in 2004. This is worth looking up so that you are aware of the standard in your state. When the emergency arises, you may not have time to conduct in-depth legal research.

> . . . (b) A lawyer may reveal a confidence or secret to the extent the lawyer reasonably believes necessary:
>
> > (1) to prevent the client from committing a criminal or fraudulent act that the lawyer believes is likely to result in death or sub-stantial bodily harm, or substantial injury to the financial in-terest or property of another . . .
>
> From the Alaska Rules of Professional Conduct

> ### WHAT DO YOU THINK?
>
> You don't work in a vacuum. You have lawyers around you. If a client is telling you that she's going to take "this here gun" (which she pulls from her handbag) and shoot her *&^%#!! boyfriend, you first have to decide if you believe her. Then you can decide which people in your firm you should talk to about it. Who's on your list? What's your approach?

To start your research, see *Rocca v. Southern Hills Counseling Center,* 671 N.E.2d 913 (Ind.App.1996).

When is your duty of confidentiality over? Not at the conclusion of the matter. Not when you don't work for that law firm anymore. Not when your client moves away or dies. You must carry the confidential information of your client with you to your grave.

Some Stuff That Happens in the Law Office Is Not Confidential

It is typical for the new paralegal's admonishment to go something like this: "Just remember that everything that goes on here in the law office is confidential." Well, that's not exactly true. The facts surrounding the smoking gun brought in by the firm's criminal defendant are confidential and therefore must not be disclosed by law firm personnel. The client's false income tax reports are also protected. The documents that show that your client breached the contract willfully and maliciously are confidences, as well. However, the lawyer standing over the paper shredder destroying those documents is not covered by the confidentiality duty. It happened in the law office, but it is not confidential. This is because: (1) The shredding is not "information gained in the representation of the client" (although you may be engaged in the representation of your client while you are standing in the doorway watching the destruction of the client's documents); (2) The shredding is criminal activity constituting the lawyer's intent to commit a fraud upon the court. Therefore, the activity of the papers being shredded is not confidential under Rule 1.6 or Rule 3.3. This shredding is a violation of some of the other rules of professional conduct, is probably a crime, as well, and should be reported to the "appropriate professional authority" under Rule 8.3 if, of course, you are in a state that has adopted Rule 8.3. So, whereas the client's documents may not be disclosed because they are covered by the duty of confidentiality, evidence of criminal activity such as the destruction of evidence should be disclosed to the appropriate authority if that's what your state law requires.

A really good Web site on confidentiality opinions from the various states is *www.legalethics.com.* The pulldown boxes are a little confusing, but you'll find lots of links there as well as the address of each state bar association.

In *U.S. v. Kovel,* 296 F.2d 918 (2d Cir. 1961), one of the first cases that extended the attorney/client privilege to a nonattorney employed by a law firm, the court used the analogy of the employment of an interpreter in order to extend the privilege to an accountant. The court said that, just as attorneys may have to employ an interpreter through whom to speak to a foreign client, they may employ an accountant to interpret complex financial matters for them. The court reasoned that both the interpreter and the accountant should be protected by the privilege because they were conduits of information between attorney and client. As a result, the accountant in *Kovel* could not be made to testify as to information given to him in confidence by a client of the attorney who employed him.

One More Time: The Attorney/Client Privilege Is Different from the Duty of Confidentiality

The attorney/client privilege will be found in your state's rules of evidence. It will say something like this: the lawyer cannot be called upon to testify as to information the client has given to the lawyer. This is true of the attorney and all nonlawyer personnel to whom the client may have divulged information.

Wigmore, in his treatise on evidence, claimed that "it has never been questioned that the privilege protects communications to the attorney's clerks and other agents."[4] It was the 1974 U.S. Supreme Court case of *Procunier v. Martinez*[5] that extended the attorney/client privilege to the paralegal for the first time. The Supreme Court in that case held that the assistance of paralegals, secretaries, outside investigators, and the like is "indispensable" to the work of an attorney, and, because communications to the attorney from the client must often be made through such assistants, the privilege must apply to them. Further, the Court also said that an unjustifiable restriction on the use of such assistants by attorneys representing prisoners was held to be an unconstitutional restriction on the right of access to the courts.

Need to know circle: Other people in the law office may be told client confidences, but only those people who "need to know." In other words, just because your friend works for the same law office, it doesn't mean that you can tell client confidences to that person. If your friend isn't working on the same case, (doesn't need to know), then confidences should not be shared.

The client who discloses to you that he killed his wife and buried her in the backyard has given you two things: confidential information <u>and</u> information that is protected by the attorney/client privilege. The first means that you cannot tell anyone (aside from your employing lawyer) what that client has said to you (even if you change the names, dates, places, or other identifying information), and the second means that you cannot be called upon to testify as to what the client said to you. If you were asked to testify, you should refuse to answer the question on the ground of attorney/client privilege.

In *People v. Mitchell,* 448 N.E.2d 121 (N.Y. 1983), the defendant, accused of murder, made disclosures to two legal secretaries and a paralegal at an attorney's law office. The court held that the attorney/client privilege did not apply but pointed out that this decision was based on the court's doubt that there was an employment contract between the defendant and the attorney and between the two secretaries and the attorney. Although this case appears to indicate that the attorney/client privilege is not extended to employees of the attorney, this case turned on the admissions of the defendant made to an attorney who had not been hired by him and to people who were not employed by the attorney. They could not, therefore, be considered "conduits" of information between attorney and client. A confession made in a common reception area will not be considered privileged because people other than the lawyer and the lawyer's agents heard.

Federal Rules of Civil Procedure Rule 26(b)(3): Work product doctrine protects from disclosure material prepared in anticipation of litigation by or for a party or by or for that party's attorney acting for his client.

Work Product Is Confidential and Privileged at the Same Time

Work product is simply the work produced by a legal professional. Some examples are research memoranda, witness interviews, and notes resulting from other investigation. A legal professional's work product is given almost absolute protection from discovery. Historically, this is because any slight factual content that such items may have is generally outweighed by the adversary system's interest in maintaining privacy of the legal professional's thought processes and in ensuring that each side relies on its own wit in preparing its respective cases. This is true of lawyers and nonlawyers alike.

TECHNOLOGY & CONFIDENTIALITY

What has the advent of the fax machine done to the concepts we have just studied? Nothing, really. The fax machine delivers the attorney letter to the client faster than the postal system. If the envelope is inadvertently addressed to opposing counsel instead of the client, what is opposing counsel's duty regarding receipt of privileged and confidential information?

> Did you know? Title III of the Omnibus Crime Control and Safe Streets Act of 1968, as amended, prohibits the interception of wire, electronic, and oral communications.

The answer depends on the jurisdiction, not how fast the information reached the wrong person. Those jurisdictions that say the receiving attorney has a duty to return the correspondence without reading it say the same thing whether the correspondence went by mail carrier, messenger, e-mail, or fax.

What has e-mail done to confidentiality? Nothing, really. Although there was a great deal of discussion about it when e-mail was new, most jurisdictions have found that breaking into your computer isn't much different from breaking into your mailbox. Stolen information is the same today as it was yesterday, only faster.

Likewise the cell phone. Again, there was a lot of discussion about cell communications not being "secure" and conversations being "stolen" out of the air. There could well be people who will use hi-tech equipment to eavesdrop on your cell communication. But these are no doubt the same people who used hi-tech equipment to bug your landline or otherwise listen in on your telephone conversations.

Should you encrypt the information on your laptop or PDA just in case they fall into enemy hands? We don't have that standard for the old-fashioned box of documents that may inadvertently be left or lost, so why would we have it for our technologically superior equipment? Until a court rules, or a state passes a law that says that we have to write our legal documents, memos, and other confidential information in code, we should not have to worry about encryption.

Should we be vigilant? Absolutely. Technology has given us more ways to communicate, so there are more opportunities for mishandling or theft of information. Has the standard changed? No.

ABA Standing Committee on Ethics and Professional Responsibility, Formal Opinion No. 99-413 (March 10, 1999): "The Committee believes that e-mail communications, including those sent unencrypted over the Internet, pose no greater risk of interception or disclosure than other modes of communication commonly relied upon as having a reasonable expectation of privacy."

At least one court has ruled that misdirected e-mail do not lose their privileged status. In *City of Reno v. Reno Police Protective Assn.,* one side came into possession of a hard copy of the other side's privileged e-mail message. The receiving party attempted to use the e-mail, claiming that the privilege had been waived by the fact that the message had been e-mailed. The Nevada Supreme Court held that the e-mail retained its privileged status and should not have been used by the other side. The court relied, in part, on ABA Formal Opinion 99-413 (1999). The court also noted that both federal and California statutes say that unlawfully intercepted electronic communications do not lose their privileged status. Here's your cite: 59 P.3d 1212 (Nev. 2002), modified, 2003 Nev. LEXIS 25 (Nev. May 14, 2003).

For an article about Wi-Fi and potential confidentiality issues, go here: *http://www.abanet.org/lpm/lpt/articles/nosearch/tch05041_print.html.*

WHAT DO YOU THINK?

Does a conversation with an attorney lose its privileged status if it is accidentally recorded? What a great case! *Jasmine Networks, Inc. v. Marvell Semiconductor, Inc.,* 117 Cal. App. 4th 794 (Cal. Ct. App. 2004).

CLIENT FILES AND CONFIDENTIALITY

Just think of all of the confidential information being stored in the file room! And what do we do with all of that stuff after the case has concluded?

We know we have a responsibility to take care of things that belong to the client that we have in our possession. The Restatement (3d) of Law Governing Lawyers requires that a lawyer "take reasonable steps to safeguard documents in the lawyer's possession relating to the representation of a client or former client."[6] This means that we can't just toss the client files in the trash or recycle bin when the case or matter has concluded. In general, we can give the files back to the client. If your firm's fee agreement specifies that the client is responsible for the files at the conclusion of the representation, with a few exceptions, we can box up the files and ship them out to the now-former client. Exceptions to this rule are certain documents that are subject to a confidentiality agreement that, by agreement, the client cannot see; certain original documents that are subject to probate or criminal code restrictions or might have to be filed with the court later; and documents that for some other reason the client should not see.

If the policy is to return all of the files to the client, the firm should consider keeping a copy for future use. If you photocopy the files so the

Maine has an April 2004 opinion on storing client files. You can find it here: *http://www.mebaroverseers.org/.*

firm can have a copy, you cannot charge the client for the copying. The files belong to the client. Any copies the firm wants to make for its own records must be done at its own expense.

If the policy is to destroy the files, you should know that most states have record retention requirements that are somewhere between five and ten years, so you should definitely find your state's requirement first. And you should check with the firm's professional liability insurance carrier. The carrier will probably tell you that you should keep the files at least for the time during which a malpractice action or breach of contract action could be filed—usually between five and ten years.

You can store the files in any secure place, although your basement probably isn't a very good idea. There are lots of inexpensive document storage facilities. And you can store files electronically.

No matter what you do, store or destroy, a comprehensive index of what the file contains should be created and kept. And, naturally, you should never destroy any document that has some intrinsic value such as money orders, travelers' checks, stocks, bonds, wills, original deeds, original notes, judgments, and the like. Also, you should never destroy documents that create or extinguish legal rights or obligations.

The ABA offered an Informal Opinion that recognized the continuing economic burden of storing retired and inactive files.[7] Sympathetically, the ABA opined that the issue of how to deal with this burden is primarily a question of business management and not of ethics or professional responsibility. However, dealing with client files is always a question of confidentiality from the file you have open on your desk to the client document carelessly put in the trash.

There is no general duty to preserve all files permanently. The public interest is not served by unnecessary additions to the costs of legal services that would be incurred by substantial storage costs. However, the ABA also concluded that clients (and former clients) reasonably expect that valuable and useful information in the lawyer's files will not be pre-

Here's an article about Delaware's position on file retention:
http://www.dsba.org/ AssocPubs/InRe/mar01et.htm.

A lawyer may comply with the mandatory record retention provision by storing certain records as computer-generated images. The lawyer must ensure that the electronic storage technique will safeguard the records from inadvertent destruction at least as effectively as the paper record, and that it will permit prompt reproduction of accurate, unaltered copies upon proper request. Before disposing any of the paper records, the lawyer must ensure that all required copies have in fact, been transferred. Certain records must be retained in their original form: check books, check stubs, bank statements, prenumbered and canceled checks, duplicative deposit slips and other documents that are not referred to as "copies."

New York State Bar Association Opinion 680 (1/10/96)

maturely and carelessly destroyed. The ABA Committee declined to state a specific time for which all files must be preserved and when those files may be destroyed. Instead, they offered that "good common sense" should provide the answers to most questions that arise regarding file retention and destruction. The committee did list some general considerations. If you are put in charge of file retention, you can read the ABA Informal Opinion 1384 (1977). (http://www.prenhall.com/orlik)

If there is no clause in your firm's fee agreement about retention of client files, which there probably isn't, and there is a need or desire to destroy these old files, many states require that you at least attempt to notify the client about the destruction of the files and the client's right to claim them. There will be technical requirements about how and when to give notice and how long you have to wait after you have not gotten a response from the former client. If the client is dead by the time you think to return his files, there will be even more requirements designed to protect the client's confidentiality requirement (which continues beyond the client's death) and any value the estate might find in the file such as continuing legal rights.

You don't have to do this the old-fashioned way. There are a number of readily available software programs to help you organize open and closed files and to put together a storage and destruction schedule.

As you have an obligation to protect the confidentiality of the client files, destruction of the files should be as complete as possible, such as by confetti shredding or burning. There is no obligation to hire a professional to destroy the documents, and destruction of the documents is not billable time. So long as the information cannot be retrieved, the confidentiality has been protected.

Here's an article about West Virginia's position on file retention from 1997: *http://www.wvbar.org/ barinfo/lawyer/APRIL97.HTM.*

And here's one from Minnesota: *http://www.courts.state.mn.us/ lprb/fc022299.html.*

RULE #2 WRAP-UP

Confidentiality is a bear. If you don't believe that most lawyers don't understand the difference between confidentiality and attorney/client privilege, run an internet search on the term "duty of confidentiality" and take a look at the numerous Web sites where some lawyer, trying to sell the public on his/her knowledge of the law, completely confuses the two concepts. Famous, brilliant lawyers who worked on the O.J. Simpson case consistently got their confidentiality confused with their attorney/client privilege. If you didn't get it the first time around on this chapter, then, don't feel bad. Just let it soak in. If you want to read some cases on this topic, some are provided for you on the publisher's Web site at *http://www.prenhall.com/orlik.*

Don't forget about the importance of confidentiality when using technology. Although the standards have not changed, the speed at which we can now communicate with each other makes it important to be more vigilant, more watchful.

And we learned about the confidential nature of client files in Rule #2. We have duties regarding these files that stem from our duty to protect the client's confidences.

RULE #2 REVIEW QUESTIONS

1. What is a short definition of "confidential information"? What are your duties under your state's law about keeping client information confidential? What client information is confidential? When does the duty begin? When does it end?

2. Compare and contrast the attorney/client privilege with the duty of confidentiality.

3. Your firm has a written fee agreement with your client. Is that fee agreement confidential? Is the fact that the client is your firm's client confidential?

4. You want to teach a class for your local paralegal program. Good! Can you use a closed file from a former firm client for your sample pleadings? How about if you black out the names and other identifying information? Why? Why not?

5. What is the "work product privilege"? What does it do for you that the attorney/client privilege does not do?

6. If you keep notes on your PDA, do you have to encrypt them?

7. What should you do with a fax transmission that is obviously confidential information and obviously not intended for you or your firm . . . in other words, it was accidentally sent to the wrong place?

8. How long must client files be kept after the client's case is concluded?

9. To whom do client files belong? What is the public policy reason for this rule?

10. What are the advantages to scanning all of the documents in client files and keeping them in electronic format? What are the disadvantages?

WHAT DO YOU THINK?

The client discloses the whereabouts of the dead bodies of his victims. What do you do with that information? Check out this case: *McClure v. Thompson,* 323 F.3d 1233 (9th Cir. April 2, 2003).

---

[1] Model Rule 1.6; EC 4-1.

[2] Paragraph (b) has two exceptions to the rule on confidentiality. The first is to prevent the client from committing a criminal act that the lawyer believes will result in death or substantial bodily harm. The second is that the lawyer can reveal certain confidences in an action to collect the fee or defend against criminal or civil charges against the lawyer based on conduct in which the client was involved or to defend a malpractice or similar claim.

[3] For an interesting article on confidentiality, see 8 Journal of Paralegal Education & Practice 1, 167 (Summer 1990).

[4] *Wigmore on Evidence,* 3d ed. (1961, Section 2290).

[5] 416 U.S. 396, 94 S.Ct. 1800 (1974).

[6] Rest.3d Law Governing Lawyers § 46(1)9(1).

[7] ABA Informal Opinion 1384 (1977).

GET AND STAY COMPETENT

The public has a right to competent professionals. This is especially true in the legal field because lawyers have traditionally been viewed in a "paternalistic" way. That is to say, members of the public traditionally did not question the lawyer's word, similar to the way they reacted to the word of doctors. Rule #3 explains what competence is in the eyes of the law and how to get and stay that way. This Rule also touches on professional negligence, even though there are no reported cases where a paralegal has been held liable for professional negligence.

WHAT THE CODES AND RULES SAY ABOUT COMPETENCE

As a testament to the importance we place on competence, it is the first section of both the ABA's Model Code and Model Rules:

> Model Code EC 1-1: A basic tenet of the professional responsibility of lawyers is that every person in our society should have ready access to the independent professional services of a lawyer of integrity and competence. Maintaining the integrity and improving the competence of the bar to meet the highest standards is the ethical responsibility of every lawyer.

> Model Rule 1.1: A lawyer shall provide competent representation to a client. Competent representation requires the legal knowledge, skill, thoroughness and preparation reasonably necessary for the representation.

So, we have a clear definition of competence from these Model Rules. Competence is having the knowledge and skill necessary for this particular representation, plus putting in the time to thoroughly prepare. The definition

NALA Code of Ethics and Professional Responsibility says at Canon 9: "A legal assistant shall work continually to maintain integrity and a high degree of competency throughout the legal profession." Canon 10 says: "A legal assistant shall strive for perfection through education in order to better assist the legal profession in fulfilling its duty of making legal services available to clients and the public."

NFPA's Model Code says:

CANON 1. A paralegal shall achieve and maintain a high level of competence.

Ethical Considerations

EC 1.1(a) A paralegal shall achieve competency through education, training, and work experience.

EC 1.1(b) A paralegal shall participate in continuing education in order to keep informed of current legal, technical and general developments.

EC 1.1(c) A paralegal shall perform all assignments promptly and efficiently.

of competence is the same for each person who works in the field of law. The NALA and NFPA Codes also cover competence.

Both of these Codes make continuing education an affirmative duty for paralegals just as Model Rule 1.1 makes continuing legal education an affirmative duty for the lawyer.

The ABA Model Rules also devote an entire rule to the lawyer's responsibilities regarding nonlawyer assistants. (Here is one of the few rules that applies exclusively to lawyers.) The ABA's position is that the employing lawyer is directly responsible for the competence of the employee paralegal.

Rule 5.3. Responsibilities Regarding Nonlawyer Assistants

With respect to a nonlawyer employed or retained by or associated with a lawyer:

(a) a partner, and a lawyer who individually or together with other lawyers possesses comparable managerial authority in a law firm, shall make reasonable efforts to ensure that the firm has in effect measures giving reasonable assurance that the person's conduct is compatible with the professional obligations of the lawyer;

The Comment that follows reaffirms that a lawyer should give appropriate training and supervision. Oddly, the Comment doesn't seem to be addressing substantive or procedural law matters so much as it addresses ethical issues.

[1] Lawyers generally employ assistants in their practice, including secretaries, investigators, law student interns, and paraprofessionals. Such assistants, whether employees or independent contractors, act for the lawyer in rendition of the lawyer's professional services. <u>A lawyer must give such assistants appropriate instruction and supervision concerning the ethical aspects of their employment</u>, particularly regarding the obligation not to disclose information relating to representation of the client, and <u>should be responsible for their work product</u>. The measures employed in supervising nonlawyers should take account of the fact that they do not have legal training and are not subject to professional discipline.

The basis for the Comment is not true, that nonlawyers do not have legal training. The second part of the Comment is not necessarily true, either, that nonlawyers are not subject to professional discipline. NFPA has a model disciplinary code in place, and several local paralegal associations are taking responsibility for disciplining their members.

Nevertheless, the Comment says that the lawyer "should be" responsible for the paralegal's work product. Other law says that the lawyer "is" responsible.

ABA Model Code EC 3-6 states:

> A lawyer often delegates tasks to clerks, secretaries, and other lay persons. Such delegation is proper if the lawyer maintains a direct relationship with his client, supervises the delegated work, and has complete professional responsibility for the work product. This delegation enables a lawyer to render legal services more economically and efficiently.

Protection of the Public Is the Goal

The rules of legal ethics are aimed at protecting the attorney/client relationship, maintaining public confidence in the legal profession, and ensuring the integrity of judicial proceedings.[1] In short, the rules are meant to protect the public.

Minimum Standards

How can we know if we are competent? The NALA Model Standards provide a list of qualifications regarding paralegal education and training. Among the listed items are graduation from an ABA approved paralegal program or a program that is accredited and requires not fewer than sixty semester hours of classroom study. In other words, the NALA standards look for graduation from a paralegal program of substance. Alternatively, graduation from a short course of study or holding a baccalaureate degree, plus in-house training as a paralegal is accepted. Of course, there are many long-term paralegals who never went to college, and they are competent, too. The NALA Standards use two years of paralegal work as a minimum.[2]

> In 2004, more than 35,000 victims initiated claims against lawyers who had legal malpractice insurance. Of those victims, 12,000 people successfully recovered money.
>
> *http://www.Legal-Malpractice-Lawyers-Attorneys.com* 2002–2004

Does education make you competent? No. But it's a good place to start when we have to draw some minimum qualification lines. We are all competent to some degree. The trick is being confident that we have the required *knowledge* and *skill* to do *this particular task* and, when we're not confident, we know when to ask for help. The problem many of us get into is when we're working alone, feel we have no one to ask, and don't realize we're in over our head.

PROFESSIONAL NEGLIGENCE

The modern trend has been to use the expression "professional negligence" rather than "malpractice" because malpractice implies a bad intent. The legal standard is really negligence, not intentional wrongdoing.

Historically, the plaintiff in a legal malpractice case had to establish that the attorney had acted in a "grossly negligent" manner toward the client.[3] More recently, however, the plaintiff in a professional negligence case only needs to establish *simple negligence* as in any other tort/negligence action. The elements of the action are these: (1) the existence of the attorney/client relationship (which gives rise to a duty); (2) acts that constitute negligence or the lack of use of reasonable skill and care; (3) the acts or omissions are the proximate cause of the damage to the client, or "but for" such negligence, the client would have been successful in his or her action; and (4) actual damages.[4]

Competence in General

A paralegal's general competence comes from education and training. Paralegals, as you have no doubt been told, are educated and trained in the "how to" of law as opposed to lawyers who learn primarily legal theory in school.

Lawyers, as members of a profession, have a bad reputation for honesty and competence. We've all heard the lawyer jokes. These jokes stem from the small minority of incompetent and dishonest lawyers. Each person's reputation reflects upon the reputation of the profession in the eyes of the public. Each negligent or dishonest act reflects badly on the individual, the supervising lawyer, the law firm, and the profession as a whole. That's why paralegals must be extra attentive to integrity (Rule #1) and competence (Rule #2) . . . so that we don't see paralegal jokes making the rounds on the Internet.

Most Legal Malpractice falls in the following classes of errors:

(1) Administrative Errors: Failure to Calendar, Failure to File/No Deadline, Clerical error, procrastination.

(2) Substantive Errors: Failure to Know Deadline, Inadequate Investigation, Failure to Know the Law, Conflict of Interest.

(3) Client Relations: Failure to Follow Client Instructions, Failure to Obtain Client's Consent, Improper Withdrawal.

(4) Intentional Wrongdoing: Libel, Malicious Prosecution, Civil Rights, Fraud, Theft.

http://www.Legal-Malpractice-Lawyers-Attorneys.com 2002–2004

Of the insured negligence claims, the most prevalent malpractice occurred in the area of personal injury—Plaintiffs (25% of all insured claims). Then came Real Estate law (16%). Probate and estate claims along with business startups (approximately 10 % each).

http://www.Legal-Malpractice-Lawyers-Attorneys.com 2002–2004

Competence in a Specific Area

Law is becoming increasingly specialized. As the law becomes more complex, it becomes harder to keep up with it. Gone are the days of the "general practitioner." Taken to an extreme, of course, the trend toward specialization would mean that the new practitioner could practice nothing, and the user of legal services would have to go to a different lawyer for each different need. But the Comments to Model Rule 1.1 say that some of the most important skills for the legal practitioner don't have anything to do with specialization or knowing any law in particular. These important skills are the ability to find the law, analysis of the law, evaluation of facts, and legal writing. To be competent, then, does not mean memorization of great bodies of law, but it does require those fundamental skills such as being able to determine what kinds of legal problems a situation may involve. Once having analyzed the problems, all of the answers are in the library. Diligence and thoroughness, coupled with analytical and drafting abilities, are the key to competence in the field of law.

To be competent in a specific area, more training and more preparation are necessary. To maintain that higher level of competence, continuing education is a must. Continuing education should be more than reading in your chosen area; it should include sharing ideas with others.

In order to become competent in a specific area, we all have to start with that first case, some extra reading and studying, and talking to others who specialize in that field, even if we have to spend more time that is

> 1,900 of the 35,000 malpractice victims were paid over $100,000 in damages.
> *http://www.Legal-Malpractice-Lawyers-Attorneys.com* 2002–2004

not billable to the client. Some sage advice: never be afraid to ask a question; never take a project unless you are qualified, unless you can get qualified or get assistance. When something is assigned to you, don't be ashamed to say: "I don't have any experience in this area."

How do we know an act (or failure to act) constitutes negligence? There is a lot of case law to guide us. The most obvious negligence is the failure to follow the law.

Lack of knowledge or nonobservance of local statutes, rules, and case law can in itself justify a finding by the court of professional negligence.[5] In *Stewart v. Sbarro,*[6] the court held that while an attorney "is not an insurer, nor is he answerable to client for every error in judgment or mistake, he contracts to use the reasonable knowledge and skill in the transaction of business which lawyers of ordinary ability and skill possess and exercise." Although *Stewart v. Sbarro* speaks of "contracts," the client's action will ordinarily be in tort . . . . as an ordinary negligence action. Punitive damages are not ordinarily available in contract actions, so the wise plaintiff includes the tort cause of action and tries to prove "gross negligence."

Although failure to follow the law seems like a clear path to a malpractice action, if the law is new or uncertain, there is perhaps no liability.[7] Laws that are clear, however, such as simple court filings, are easy pickings for a malpractice action. For example, in *DeBakey v. Staggs,*[8] the lawyer was hired to have the clients' daughter's name changed. The attorney filed the necessary papers only after being badgered by the clients, and his papers were not signed by the court because of several defects. After seven months of urging the attorney to complete the job (for which he had been partially paid), the clients hired another attorney to perform the name change. In the lawsuit against the original attorney, the clients were awarded treble damages[9] under the state Deceptive Trade Practices Act and $1,000 attorney's fees for the professional negligence action.

Examples of Negligence

Statute of limitations is the length of time between the bad thing happening and the filing of the lawsuit that the law allows. Most states have statutes of limitations that allow one year for negligence actions and up to four years on contract actions.

Legal professionals will be liable for any loss sustained by their client as a result of their negligent failure to prepare, file, or serve the appropriate pleadings.[10] If the case is never filed, and the *statute of limitations* runs, how can the injured client prove losses? In *Gyler v. Mission Insurance Co.,*[11] the court held that the attorney's failure to file a suit before the statute of limitations has run on the action is "plainly malpractice where the attorney can show no reasonable justification for his inaction." But, the Illinois Appellate Court held that the plaintiff has to show that "but for" the attorneys' negligence in allowing the statute to run, the plaintiff would have won his or her case.[12] In essence, this rule forces the plaintiff not only to show negligence on the part of the attorney but also to sustain the burden of proof on the underlying action. Because the underlying action was never litigated and therefore no discovery was ever gathered, this burden is a difficult one.

WHAT DO YOU THINK?

Should an attorney be found negligent for not taking a case? If the attorney fails to do the minimum research before telling the client that there is no cause of action in her complaints, should he be liable for her failure to seek out another opinion? What if he also fails to tell her about the running of the statute of limitations? Has an attorney/client relationship been established? You can start your research with *Dogstad v. Veseley, Otto, Miller & Keefe,* 291 N.W.2d 686 (Minn. 1980).

In *Kotzur v. Kelly,*[13] purchasers in a real estate transaction brought a malpractice action against the seller's attorney after they were forced to pay off a judgment lien against the seller following the closing. The attorney argued that because he was never employed to represent the purchasers, no attorney/client relationship existed, and no cause of action for legal malpractice could be brought. The attorney testified that he didn't feel that he was dealing with two different parties and that he knew that the purchasers did not have a separate attorney. He prepared all the documents relating to the sale transaction for the purchasers on a "family-type basis." The purchasers thought that the attorney was handling the

---

In *Wells v. State Bar,* 575 P.2d 285 (Cal. 1978), the client was indicted when he refused to submit to the military draft regulations. His attorney persuaded him to enlist in the military and subsequently file a petition for conscientious objector status. Although criminal charges against the client were dropped when he enlisted, they were reinstated shortly thereafter when he was absent without leave in order to prepare his own c.o. petition, after having gotten no action on his matter from his attorney. The client was in constant communication with the attorney, but each contact resulted in the attorney's litany of excuses. The client eventually submitted his own petition and was released from the service three weeks later. The Supreme Court of California held that Attorney Wells's habitual disregard of his client's needs and his virtual abandonment of his client were clearly professional negligence.

documents and that he was representing them. Purchasers' testimony was that the attorney did not tell them that he was not representing them nor did he tell them that it would be better if they hired a separate lawyer. The court found the existence of an attorney/client relationship for purposes of the malpractice action.

Negligent Disregard for the Client

Lack of communication with clients is a problem of growing concern to the state bars. Recent polls show that among the top three client complaints is this: "My attorney doesn't communicate with me." An increasing number of attorneys accept the representation of more clients than they can conceivably represent competently, and that often means neglecting some clients in favor of others. Paralegals can assist their lawyer-employers, help the clients, and promote good public relations by keeping clients informed. Clients need to know the important developments in their cases. They need the procedural steps explained to them. They are entitled to explanations for delays. Their telephone calls and letters should be responded to in a timely fashion. With proper supervision and direction, paralegals and other nonlawyer assistants can and should do all of these tasks.

Good Faith as a Defense

If, however, the legal professional acts in good faith with an honest belief that his or her acts and advice are in the client's best interest and that they are based on accurate information and adequate research, the legal professional will not be liable for mere errors in judgment. In *In re Watts,*[14] it was specifically held that innocent error does not violate the attorney's fiduciary duty and to hold otherwise would offend the independence of the bar.

WHAT DO YOU THINK?

Should a lawyer be disbarred for repeatedly abusing drugs? To start your research, look for *The Florida Bar v. Heptner,* _____ So.2d _____, 29 Fla.L.Weekly S495 (Fla., Nos. SC01-1298, SC02-1118, 9/15/2004).

Standard of Care

Generally, the standard of care is "such skill, prudence, and diligence as lawyers of ordinary skill and capacity commonly possess and exercise in the performance of tasks which they undertake."[15] However, where attorneys hold themselves out to the public as specialists in areas of law, they will be held to the same standard of care and skill as that of other specialists of ordinary ability who specialize in the same fields.[16] In *Wright v.*

Williams,[17] the court held that attorneys who held themselves out to the public as specialists in maritime law should be held to the standard of care of a "reasonably prudent specialist" in that field. The court allowed expert testimony of other maritime law specialists in order to determine if the defendant/attorney breached the duty he owed to his clients.

Statute of Limitations in Negligence Actions

The statute of limitations on ordinary negligence cases begins to run at the time of the negligent act. With professional negligence, however, it is conceivable that the injured party will not become aware of the problem until many years after the attorney's representation has ended. For that reason, some courts have held that in cases of negligent drawing of a will, the statute should begin to run at the time of the testator's death.[18] Problems arise with this theory when it takes many years for a will to be probated. The statute could run without the injured party ever having discovered the negligence of the legal professional.

In *Neel v. Magana, Olney, Levy, Cathart & Gelfand,*[19] the court held that the "discovery" theory for beginning the statute of limitations in attorney negligence cases is most appropriate. In other words, the statute of limitations on the action does not begin to run until the client has discovered, or a reasonable person should have discovered, the negligence, error, or omission. In *Johnson v. Simonelli,*[20] the client brought an action against his former attorney for legal malpractice claiming that the attorney did not ensure that adequate security existed for a debt owed to the client arising out of the sale of the client's business. The court held that the statute of limitations began to run at the time of the buyer's default. Citing *Neel,* the court said:

This is often called "the discovery rule."

> The statute of limitations in a legal malpractice action does not begin to run until the client <u>discovers, or should have discovered</u>, the attorney's negligence and the client has sustained actual and appreciable harm.

Another problem in this area is that of privity of contract. Where the negligence claimant has actually employed the attorney or has consulted with the attorney in contemplation of retaining the attorney, the privity of contract is clear. The problem arises where the heirs of a client allege that the attorney performed legal services for the testator in a negligent manner. In that case, the person in privity of contract is dead and it is this person's heirs who want to sue the attorney. Where the plaintiff is an heir of the decedent, the plaintiff is not the one who hired the attorney and has no *fiduciary relationship* with the attorney. Some states require that the person bringing a malpractice action be in direct privity of contract with the lawyer.[21] Other states do not. If no privity is required, the beneficiaries of a will, for example, become "hidden" parties in the attorney/client contract. This creates more people to whom the legal professional owes the duty of competence.[22]

A *"fiduciary relationship"* is one founded on trust or confidence placed by one person in the integrity and fidelity of another.

PROFESSIONAL NEGLIGENCE LIABILITY INSURANCE

Lawyers' professional liability insurance (also known as errors and omissions or E&O insurance) became available after World War II. Before that time, only Lloyds of London would underwrite a policy for any professional other than a doctor. Because of the increasingly complex nature of the law and legal practice, compounded by the fact that cases handled by lawyers involve increasingly large amounts of money, professional liability insurance has become a standard expense of the practicing lawyer. Some states require that a lawyer disclose his or her liability insurance (or lack thereof) in each retainer agreement so that the client can make an informed choice.

Professional liability insurance is now available to paralegals. Policies look very much like policies for attorneys and have similar coverage. The rates, however, are substantially less. This may be because the potential liability of a paralegal, who primarily works for a lawyer, is lower than the potential liability of the lawyer. If, indeed, the doctrine of *respondeat superior* still protects the negligent paralegal, what is the need for insurance? Here's the need: many lawyers don't have professional liability insurance. There is no law that requires them to have it (except in Oregon). Whether or not the paralegal is negligent, he or she may well be sued. Even if the paralegal is not found liable, professional liability insurance will protect the paralegal from prohibitively high defense costs. As there have been instances of paralegals being named as defendants in malpractice suits in the 1990s, this type of insurance is something to think about.

Respondeat superior is Latin for "let the master answer."

Freelance paralegals may more likely have potential liability, as they may not be covered by an attorney's policy, and the attorney-employer may not have liability insurance. Those who walk the dangerous line between typing services and practicing law without a license should also think seriously about this kind of insurance. Legal technicians, authorized to practice in limited areas, should look at professional liability insurance. You can be held liable for legal malpractice even if you are not licensed to practice law,[23] although it is unlikely that you can be insured for malpractice if you are not authorized to engage in the activity in which the malpractice was committed.

Additionally, independent insurance coverage may make you more desirable when you are looking for a job. In any case, it is a good idea to find out if your employer has liability insurance and look into your own if you are not otherwise covered.

Ordinarily, professional liability insurance covers direct monetary loss and expense to the legal professional or a firm that arise from claims of neglect, omissions, or errors. This type of insurance does not cover bodily injury or property damage and will compensate only for loss that actually "arises from" the conduct of professional legal services.[24] Professional liability insurance usually does not compensate for intentional torts, only negligence.

Paralegal/Law Errors & Omissions

Coverage is arranged for errors and omissions for paralegals and law clerks, either as part of an attorney's professional liability package or as a separate E&O form under various programs. E&O limits range from $100,000 per claim and $300,000 aggregate on claims-made forms to $1 million/$1 million. Premiums and limits are lower for paralegals who work under the supervision of an attorney.

Model Rule 1.8(h) and EC 6-6 say that lawyers must not attempt to limit their liability for professional negligence by contract with their client, but attorneys who are members of a professional legal corporation may limit their responsibility for the professional negligence of their associates to the extent permitted by law.

LIABILITY FOR OTHERS

A law partnership, as well as all its members, is liable for the negligent acts of the individual members of the firm performed within the scope of their authority,[25] but not for acts committed outside of the course of business.[26] The firm will not be held liable for the negligent acts of a partner that are committed outside of his or her position with the firm. Limited liability partnerships (LLPs) have proliferated in the 1990s in an attempt to narrow the scope of law firm liability.

Model Rule 5.3(a) and Ethical Consideration 4-2 advise the attorney to exercise due care in the selection of competent and trustworthy persons to conduct the affairs of the attorney's clients. Under the doctrine of *respondeat superior,* attorneys will be held liable for the negligent acts of their nonattorney employees if those acts occur during the course and within the scope of their employment. Further, attorneys will be held negligent themselves for improperly supervising all of their nonattorney personnel. In *Black v. State Bar,*[27] the California Supreme Court ruled that, although the attorney could not be held to have knowledge of every small detail of his office, he must accept responsibility for the supervision of the work of his staff.

Although a paralegal may draft all the pleadings and papers necessary to be drawn for the attorney's practice,[28] the attorney is responsible for examining those papers, approving them, or altering them to meet the standards of due care and diligence of an ordinary attorney of like skill and knowledge.[29]

The standard of care used to determine negligence on the part of a paralegal will probably be that of a reasonable paralegal under the circumstances. When people represent themselves as having even greater skill than that of the ordinary person, they will be held to that higher standard. Since paralegals are engaged in a specific profession, they will be held to the standard higher than that of the ordinary person: that of a person of their training and abilities and of the type of professional they hold themselves out to be. There is no case law on this at this time. The best guess, then, would be that paralegals will be held to a standard lower than that of an attorney, but higher than that of the layperson.

Whereas attorneys may not be held liable for a "mere error of judgment" to avoid liability under a negligence theory,[30] since paralegals are not supposed to use legal judgment, this theory may not be available to them. As yet, it is difficult to determine what "customary practice" may be for paralegals; thus, that professional negligence defense is eliminated as well. It may be that once they step outside of their limited realm of practice, paralegals will be held to the standard of the full professional, in spite of their inability to utilize that standard in their daily interaction with clients and the courts.

Per se
is a Latin expression
meaning "by itself."

To clarify this problem, take the example of the paralegal who may be found to be engaging in the unauthorized practice of law. If the court finds that a violation of prescribed standards amounts to negligence *per se*, then this paralegal may be found negligent per se. On the other hand, many courts have been reluctant to use the per se theory when the standard breached is one of licensing. It can be reasoned, then, that if a license is the only thing between a paralegal and an attorney, these courts would find that license insufficient for a per se holding.

However, courts have not found that the only difference between a layperson and an attorney is the license, but rather, also the specialized training and skill. The paralegal is somewhere in between the two, with some specialized training and skill, but not quite that of an attorney. The answer to the per se question, then, is this: maybe.

Some jurisdictions have held that the compelling reason for licensing statutes is protection of the public from the sort of injury caused by the unlicensed person; thus, the incompetence of the particular defendant is of no consequence. In *Biakanja v. Irving*,[31] a layman improperly prepared certain documents that were subsequently declared unenforceable. His conduct was clearly negligent, but the court muddied the issues by making the point that the defendant was practicing law without a license, which may have led the court to a negligence per se holding. In *Matter of Laclas*,[32] however, the court held that the unauthorized practice of law did not per se void all proceedings. The court remanded the issue for an investigation into the adequacy of the representation.

RULE #3 WRAP-UP

Some rules of thumb on competence are:

1. Keep abreast of changes in the law. Take continuing education classes. Read legal journals and periodicals.

2. Hold yourself out as a specialist in a field only if you have worked in that field for a substantial length of time or have a specialist certificate in that field.

3. Be completely honest about what you know how to do and what you do not know how to do. If you are unsure of your skills, be sure that you are working in a place where you will get training and supervision.

4. Keep in mind that your loyalties must be to your firm, supervising attorney, paralegal supervisor, and your firm's clients. Don't let outside influences affect the quality of your work.

5. As soon as you notice a problem, such as a missed statute of limitations or other serious error, bring it to the attention of your supervisor.

6. Never, under any circumstances, try to hide a potential ethical or legal problem.

RULE #3 REVIEW QUESTIONS

1. What is "competence"? Why is it important to the legal profession to be competent?

2. What duties does a lawyer have regarding the duty of the paralegal to be competent?

3. What is the primary goal of the competence requirements?

4. List some of the requirements for paralegal competence provided by the paralegal associations.

5. Why do we use the expression "professional negligence" rather than the expression "malpractice"?

6. What does the Latin expression "*respondeat superior*" mean?

7. Who is responsible for the errors of one lawyer or paralegal in a firm of many lawyers?

8. What is the ordinary standard of care? When is a higher standard of care used?

9. Do you think that licensing paralegals would generally improve paralegal competence?

10. What are some of the things each paralegal can do to ensure competence?

---

[1] *SK Handtool Corp. v. Dresser Industries,* 619 N.E.2d 1282 (Ill.App. 1993).

[2] NALA Model Standards and Guidelines. This is taken from the NALA Website at *http://www. nala.org.*

[3] *Pearson v. Darrington,* 32 Ala. 227 (1858).

[4] *Christy v. Saliterman,* 179 N.W.2d 288 (Minn. 1970).

[5] *George v. Caton,* 600 P.2d 822 (N.M. 1979), *cert. quashed,* 98 P.2d 215.

6   At 586, quoted from *McCullough v. Sullivan*, 132 A. 102 (N.J. 1925) [362 A.2d 581 (N.J. 1976)]

7   *Medrano v. Miller*, 608 S.W.2d 81 (Tex. 1980).

8   605 S.W.2d 631 (Tex. Civ. App.—Houston [1st Dist.] 1980).

9   The difference between DeBakey's fee and the fee they paid the other attorney tripled.

10 *Goebel v. Lauderdale*, 214 Cal.App.3d 1502, 263 Cal.Rptr. 275 (1989); *Smith v. Lewis*, 530 P.2d 589 (Cal. 1975).

11 514 P.2d 1219 (Cal. 1973).

12 *Connaughton v. Gertz*, 418 N.E.2d 858 (Ill.App. 1981).

13 791 S.W.2d 254 (Tex.1990).

14 190 U.S. 1, 23 S.Ct. 718 (1903).

15 *Ishmael v. Millington* (3rd Dist. 1966) 241 Cal.App.2d 520, at 523.

16 *Rodriguez v. Horton*, 622 P.2d 261 (N.M. 1980).

17 47 Cal.App.3d 802, 121 Cal.Rptr. 194 (1975).

18 *Millright v. Romer*, 322 N.W.2d 30 (Iowa 1982).

19 491 P.2d 421 (Cal. 1971).

20 231 Cal.App.3d 105, 282 Cal.Rptr. 205 (1991).

21 *Robinson v. Benton*, 842 So. 2d 631 (Ala. 2002); *Noble*, 709 A.2d at 1275; *Lilyhorn v. Dier*, 335 N.W.2d 554, 555 (Neb. 1983); *Mali v. De Forest & Duer*, 553 N.Y.S.2d 391, 392 (N.Y. App. Div. 1990); *Simon v. Zipperstein*, 512 N.E.2d 636, 638 (Ohio 1987); *Barcelo v. Elliot*, 923 S.W.2d 575 (Tex. 1996).

22 California leads the pack here. See *Lucas v. Hamm*, 364 P.2d 685 (Cal. 1961), *cert. denied*, 368 U.S. 987 (1962). See also: Bradley E.S. Fogel, *Attorney v. Client—Privity, Malpractice and the Lack of Respect for the Primacy of the Attorney-Client Relationship in Estate Planning*, 68 Tenn. L. Rev. 261, 311–24 (2001).

23 *Busch v. Flangas*, 837 P.2d 438 (Nev. 1992).

24 Stern & Rottman, *Purchasing Lawyer Malpractice Insurance*, 19 Prac.Law. 29 (1973).

25 *Allen v. Frawley*, 82 N.W. 593 (Wis. 1900).

26 *Blackmon v. Hale*, 463 P.2d 418 (Cal. 1970).

27 499 P.2d 968 (Cal. 1972).

28 *Johnson v. Davidson*, 202 Cal.Rptr. 159 (1921).

29 *Ferris v. Snively*, 19 P.2d 942 (Wash. 1933).

30 *Hodges v. Carter*, 80 S.E.2d 144 (N.C. 1954).

31 310 P.2d 63 (Cal.App. 1957).

32 410 N.Y.S.2d 307 (1978).

CHARGE ONLY FAIR FEES

Even though we typically refer to law as a "profession," it is also a business. Just as with any other business, one objective is to make a profit. The fee agreement with a client, then, is the place where we balance the cost of that client's case and the amount of money that can be generated by that case so that the firm makes a profit. It may be lore that fee agreements have nothing to do with paralegals. You have likely been told that paralegals cannot "make fee agreements" or "negotiate fee agreements" with clients. However, as a billable employee, you are part of the fee chain and have the ethical obligation to be fair. Here we go.

FEE AGREEMENTS WITH CLIENTS

Fee agreements are typically not negotiated between the client and the lawyer, but they should be. In the vast majority of instances, the law firm has a standard fee agreement that the client just signs without reading. It's not unlike buying a car. Did we read all of those documents? No, of course not. The sales agent explained the big points of the deal (cost of the car, the interest rate, and penalties) and showed us where to sign. And we signed. It's only after there's a problem that we read the fine print. But the car dealership is not under a duty to explain the contract to the consumer. The lawyer is. Furthermore, the more open communication there is between the law firm and the client at the inception of the case, the less likely there will be disputes later about the attorney's bills. The legal fee must not only be fully explained to the client but also must be *objectively reasonable*. If it is not a reasonable agreement, the court will not enforce it. ABA Model Rule 1.5 lists factors to be considered in determining the reasonableness of a fee. Included in this list are things like the time and work required on the matter, the novelty and difficulty of the issues, and the fee customarily charged for this work. Your state has probably adopted a list of factors for determining reasonableness of fees. Now would be a good time to locate that law.

Objectively reasonable: Reasonable in the minds of all people, not distorted by personal feelings or interpretation.

> What's the law in your state on fee agreements? Do they have to be in writing? To begin your research, try West's Digest Topic "Attorney & Client," key number 142.

UPL is Rule #7.

Paralegals are not permitted to "negotiate" fee agreements with clients on behalf of a lawyer.[1] The rationale for this rule is that the **negotiation** (i.e., bargaining) of a fee agreement is the unauthorized practice of law (UPL). However, just as there are exceptions to UPL standards, there is an exception to this rule: that is where the paralegal is explaining a routine fee agreement to a client. In other words, if the agreement is not "negotiated," that is, if the client agrees to the contract as it is written, there is arguably nothing UPL-ish with having the contract explained by the paralegal or having the client sign the agreement without discussing it with an attorney. If the paralegal has been given instruction in the various elements of the contract and told to explain it to the client, this cannot constitute "the unauthorized practice of law," as the paralegal is doing nothing more than repeating what the lawyer said. (See Rule #7 for a discussion of "conduit of information.") We are balancing the need for the client to thoroughly understand the fee agreement against society's concerns regarding UPL and the need to have an efficient, cost-effective law practice.

Live in Florida? Check out *www.sunethics.com* for up-to-date ethics information in that state.

Paralegals in most firms are viewed as **billable;** that is, the time they spend on a legal matter is billed to the client. It is helpful to be aware of the fee agreement that the law firm has with each client so that you can bill in accordance with the agreement. However, some law firms keep these fee agreements as closely held secrets. Additionally, the agreement with the client is a **confidential communication,** so it should not be discussed with anyone outside of the law firm.

In fact, that a particular person is the client of the firm is confidential.

Contingency Fees

There are many different kinds of fee agreements: contingency, hourly, mixed billing, and value billing are just some of them. The plaintiff's side of most personal injury cases is taken on a **contingency fee** basis. This means that the law firm's recovery of legal fees is *contingent* upon the outcome of the case. The law firm may advance the costs of the lawsuit as well as dedicate hours to it. At the end of the lawsuit, if the judgment (or settlement) is in favor of the plaintiff, the law firm and the client will split the money. The expenses must be paid, as well. Expenses can include costs of litigation (such as filing fees, deposition costs, and expert witness fees) as well as costs pertaining to medical treatment of the plaintiff. Who pays these expenses and out of what money are two of the things that should be negotiated between the firm and the client.

Contingent means dependent on conditions or occurrences not yet established.

Let's take some examples:

Suppose that the client and the defendant have agreed to a $100,000 settlement amount.

Assuming the lawyer has a 40% contingency fee, spent $10,000 in costs, and the client's hospital bills total $30,000, the $100,000 could be apportioned like this:

$40,000 to the lawyer.

$60,000 to the client, but out of the client's portion, subtract $10,000 in costs (paid back to the lawyer) and hospital bills (paid to the hospital) of $30,000. Now the client has $20,000 remaining.

The $100,000 could be divided like this:

$10,000 in costs (paid back to the lawyer).

$36,000 (40% of $90,000) to the lawyer, leaving $54,000 for the client from which he must pay $30,000 to the hospital. Now the client ultimately gets $26,000.

The $100,000 could be divided like this:

$30,000 to the hospital.

$10,000 in costs (paid back to the lawyer), leaving $60,000; the lawyer gets 40% ($24,000), and the client gets the remaining $36,000.

As you can see, the method of calculating the fees can make a big difference in the amount the client will ultimately get from the lawsuit. This is why a careful and complete explanation of the fee agreement is important. The more the client understood and agreed to, the more likely the contract will be affirmed.[2]

Lawyers have been known to "overreach" in contingency fee agreements so that they are getting more than their fair share. For example, a contingency fee agreement allocating 20% to the client and 80% to the lawyer is overreaching. Even if the fee agreement is completely and carefully explained to the client, a fee that is objectively unfair will not be permitted. In determining the fairness of the contract, the court will look at the sophistication of the client, how well the contract was explained to the client by the law firm, and how acceptable the fee agreement would seem to the average person.

An infamous California civil rights attorney, after winning $44,000 in punitive damages for his clients, asked for and received $378,000 in attorney's fees under the federal civil rights statute 42 USC§ 1988. But the attorney did not tell the U.S. district court that he had a fee agreement with his clients that entitled him to 45 percent of their damage award. The fee agreement also provided that the costs of the litigation would be deducted from the clients' 55 percent. This left the clients, who had suffered a substantial loss, about $800 each. The State Bar of California found that the attorney had taken an unconscionable fee. The double fee was "objectively unreasonable and unfair."

Model Rule 1.5 provides for contingent fee agreements to be in writing and to fully set forth who gets what and in what order under the agreement. Most states have similar rules. The law in most states also provides that a contingency agreement is not permitted in some family law matters and all criminal matters.

Hourly Billing

Another method of billing, and probably the most widely used in personal injury defense and every other kind of legal representation, is **hourly billing.** When each billable person begins working at a law firm, he or she will be assigned a certain **billing rate.** You should ask what your billing rate will be just so that you will have an idea of what an hour of your time is worth (and so that you know, if you have an urge to cheat on your time sheets, how much you are cheating the client).

If your firm uses hourly billing, all billable employees (attorneys, law clerks, and paralegals, usually) will be asked to keep an account of the time spent on each task and for what client. For purposes of illustration, the smallest billable amount is 1/10 of an hour, or 6 minutes. In this illustration, the paralegal's billing rate is $100 per hour and the attorney's billing rate is $250 per hour.

As a paralegal, you may be asked to keep a daily time log like this one that accounts for all of your time for each of the clients or cases you work on.

Over a period of one month, your time records and the time records of all billers on this client's matter will be put together on one account statement.

These time records are compiled by an accounting staff member, bookkeeper, or an outside service and sent to the client in a form that looks like this:

This itemized bill allows the client to see who is working on his case, what each person is doing, and how much time is being spent. Years ago, the client would be sent a bill that looked like this:

 Law Office of John B. Davis
1234 Oak Avenue
Anytown, OH
404/555-1212

July 1, 2005
Mr. Charles J. Dolan
50 Tower Road
Anytown, OH

Re: Dolan v. State of Ohio—services through June 30, 2005

FOR SERVICES RENDERED   **$10,625.75**

But those days are over. State laws across the country now require enough detail to keep the client informed. Even if the law did not require it, clients, who have gotten more sophisticated over the years, would demand it.

There are lots of software programs that make this happen in the modern law office. Your daily time records may well be kept on a computer program so that they can be automatically integrated into the time records of the other billers. Before any bill gets sent to the client, however, an attorney responsible for that client reviews the bill. At this point, the responsible attorney has an opportunity to see if the bill looks as if it is too high considering the work that was performed, if any discounts should be given, or if someone spent too much time doing some task. At this point, that responsible attorney will "write down" time or, in some instances, "write up" time.

DAILY TIME SHEET

Date 06/24/05

Employee Renee A. Marcus—Paralegal

TIME	MATTER	DESCRIPTION
.3	Jones	telephone call to Secretary of State for corporate status check
.5	Dolan	draft letter to Dept. of Motor Vehicles regarding Mr. Dolan's driving record
.75	Dolan	research case law on driving/negligence
1.5	Jones	research client's employment record
2	Smith	track down previous students to provide information/references of Mr. Smith's teaching method
5.05	**TOTAL**	

DAILY TIME SHEET

Date ___06/25/05___

Employee ___John B. Davis—attorney___

TIME	MATTER	DESCRIPTION
.1	Dolan	telephone call to Dept of Defense to verify Mr. Dolan's release from the Army
.5	Smith	draft letter to Board of Education regarding Mr. Smith's work record and job performance
.7	Black	review file to look for copy of client's birth certificate
3.5	Dolan	review deposition summary of Accident Witness #1
.6	Dolan	review RAMs mark-up of draft letter and make appropriate revisions; put in final form
2.2	White	deposition summary/ Mr. Witness
7.6	**TOTAL**	

WHAT DO YOU THINK?

An attorney catches you in the hallway and says, "Quick! I need to know where the state's legal rate of interest is." You run on down the hall to the library. Unfortunately, you look and look and can't find the darned thing . . . but eventually you do. It took you five hours, and there it was, all along, in the state constitution. You have to account for your time. What do you do? What's fair to the client? Should the client be charged for 5 hours if it should have taken 30 minutes to find the answer?

Law Office of John B. Davis
MONTHLY TIME SHEET

Date   06/01/05–06/30/05

Client   Charles J. Dolan

TIME	DATE	INIT	DESCRIPTION
.5	06/24/05	RAM	draft letter to Dept. of Motor Vehicles regarding Mr. Dolan's driving record
.75	06/24/05	RAM	research case law on driving/negligence
.1	06/25/05	JBD	telephone call to Dept. of Defense
3.5	06/25/05	JBD	review deposition summary of Accident Witness #1
.6	06/25/05	JBD	reviewed RAMs mark-up draft letter and made revisions; put in final form
~~.25~~	~~06/28/05~~	~~RAM~~ *JBD*	~~set up appointment to meet with arresting officer~~
1.5	06/30/05	JBD	review deposition summary/officer
6.95	**TOTAL**		

Other Billing Methods

Another approach to billing is **value billing.** This describes an agreement with the client whereby the client will be charged a flat rate for certain tasks. For example, if your fee agreement says that the client will be billed $150 for each complaint that is drafted on his or her behalf, this is value billing. If the client knows that interrogatories are $200 and court appearances are $500, he or she has a better idea of how much each matter will cost because the value billing cost is not dependent on the time it takes each individual to accomplish a task.

In some places, value billing refers to the contract under which the law firm gets paid a small amount for the work done and a bonus for a good result. In other words, the client is willing to pay more when he or she wins. Some people also refer to this kind of arrangement as **bonus billing.**

Law Office of John B. Davis

1234 Oak Avenue
Anytown, OH
404/555-1212

July 1, 2005
Mr. Charles J. Dolan
50 Tower Road
Anytown, OH

Re: Dolan v. State of Ohio—services through June 30, 2005

DATE	DESCRIPTION	INIT	TIME	RATE	TOTAL
06/24	draft letter to DMV	RAM	.5	$75	$37.50
06/24	research case law	RAM	.75	$75	$56.25
06/24	review files and arrest record	RAM	1.5	$75	$112.50
06/25	telephone call	JBD	.1	$150	$15.00
06/25	review of deposition summaries	JBD	3.5	$150	$525.00
06/25	draft letter to DMV	JBD	.6	$150	$90.00
06/30	depostion summary	JBD	1.5	$150	$225.00

TOTAL NOW DUE   **$1061.25**

If you have any questions or concerns about this bill, please call
immediately and ask to speak with Janice in Accounting.

WHAT DO YOU THINK?

Morris Green died on March 3, 2004, allegedly as the result of a beat-
ing by Detroit police officers. His widow filed a wrongful death action
and was very quickly offered $5.25 million to settle. Even though her
attorney had done very little work, his fee agreement entitled him to
$1.7 million. Should he get that amount of money for filing a complaint?
Is that fair?

A cousin to value billing is **fixed fee billing.** This is an arrangement
with the client whereby the client is charged one flat rate for the repre-

sentation regardless of how long it takes or how much work is involved. In representations that are mass-produced, such as relief from stay in bankruptcy or consumer collection matters, fixed fee billing is very popular. It allows the client to budget legal fees from the beginning of the representation; it encourages efficiency; it encourages delegation of work to employees who are more suited to the tasks; and it provides training for new staff members in an atmosphere where "hours billed" is not the primary focus. In essence, the client is paying for a product.

WHAT DO YOU THINK?

The state of New York filed a class action lawsuit against the tobacco industry in 1997. In 2002, the case had ended and the six law firms representing the state filed a motion for their unprecedented $625 million fee. The judge in charge of the case said that the fee didn't pass the "smell test." Does it? What factors would you consider if you were the judge?

A variation of the typical hourly billing system is **blended rate billing.** In this arrangement, rather than paying $250 an hour for the partner, $180 an hour for the associate, and $75 an hour for the paralegal, the client agrees to pay one hourly rate, a blended rate of, for example, $150 an hour, for all billing employees. This encourages the firm to utilize the lower rate billers and to use the expensive partners sparingly.

Other Fee Agreement Terms

To ensure that it is paid, the law firm will often require a **retainer** from the client. Retainers can be confusing, but it is vital that the client understand what kind of agreement is being made.

The **classic retainer** insures the attorney's availability over time; it is considered earned upon receipt, whether or not services are actually provided. For example, if you are O.J. Simpson, you might call your friend Robert Shapiro from Chicago and say, "I'm coming home soon. I need you to clear your calendar for me. Don't take any cases in the next few days." Bob says to him, "Well, okay, but I need to take cases so that I can make a living, so if you want me to keep my calendar clear, you need to pay me for that." O.J. wires him $10,000 to keep him "on retainer," or available.

Another type of retainer that is earned upon receipt regardless of services actually rendered is sometimes called a **nonrefundable retainer.** Some courts have declared nonrefundable retainers per se unreasonable because the client has an absolute right to fire the lawyer for any reason at any time. A nonrefundable retainer impairs that right. A nonrefundable retainer has also been condemned as an unearned fee.

WHAT DO YOU THINK?

Your friend is accused of cheating and is dismissed from school. She hires a lawyer who asks for a nonrefundable retainer. The agreement states that the lawyer will try to get your friend back into school because, of course, no one can guarantee a positive result. After the agreement is signed and the money is paid, the lawyer calls the dean of the school, explains your friend's innocence, and asks the dean to reinstate her. The dean says no. Okay, says the lawyer, I tried but can't get you back in. Has the fee been earned? Is it fair for the lawyer to keep the entire fee?

An **advance payment retainer** is present payment compensating the attorney for services to be performed in the future; it is considered earned upon receipt and may be a "flat fee," in other words, it may be paid without expectation that there will be future compensation sought once the retainer is exhausted.

The more common type of retainer is a **security retainer.** Its purpose is to secure payment for future services. Technically, the security retainer remains the property of the client until applied to charges for services actually rendered, and any unused portion is refundable to the client. This is the most typical kind of retainer used in hourly billing situations. When you hear your office co-workers talking about a retainer, this is probably what they are talking about.

It works like this: the client may give the law firm a $10,000 retainer by way of a check. This money is deposited into the Client Trust Account (as opposed to a general operating account of the law firm), and is drawn against as the firm bills the client. So, at the end of the month, the firm sends the client a bill for $2,300. If the client does not object to any parts of the bill, the firm may take that $2,300 out of the $10,000 sitting in the Client Trust Account. When the $10,000 is nearly depleted, the firm may

Law Firm Spotlight: Lindquist & Vennum, a firm of 175 lawyers and 30 paralegals, has two offices: one in Denver and another in Minneapolis. L&V boasts 100 percent of its lawyers and paralegals meet or exceed the ABA's pro bono hours challenge. Proving that law firms can help in the community in more ways than one, L&V formed the Winter Closet Foundation in 2002. The Foundation provides warm clothes for children in the Denver and Minneapolis regions. All the clothes are new and purchased by employees of the firm. The Winter Closet initiative was the key reason L&V was a recipient of the Minneapolis Regional Chamber of Commerce's 2003 Quality of Life Award. You can find L&V at http://www.lindquist.com.

ask the client to replenish it. Alternatively, the firm may look to the client to actually pay (write a new check for) the $2,300. The $10,000 stays on deposit in the Client Trust Account just in case the client does not pay that bill and some future bills. The $10,000, then, is a cushion so that the firm can be sure that its bills will be paid.

The firm, of course, has many clients, so the money in the Client Trust Account is a compilation of the retainers from all of these different clients. It is one account but it has the retainer money from all of the firm's clients in it. Each client's money can be used to pay the expenses of each client's case, but must never be used to pay for another client's case, the operating expenses of the law firm, or the personal expenses of any of the lawyers or employees. The sanctity of the Client Trust Account is discussed under Rule #10.

PRO BONO WORK

While we're talking about fees, we should talk about working for no fee. This is called *pro bono work*. Pro bono work is a big part of making legal services available to the public. Model Rule 1.5 and Ethical Consideration 2-16 say that reasonable fees should be charged to the client in appropriate cases in which the clients are able to pay them. Nevertheless, under Model Rule 6.1, persons who are unable to pay reasonable fees should be able to obtain necessary legal services. To ensure that all people can get legal assistance when they need it, legal professionals should "support and participate in ethical activities designed to achieve that objective." This is covered in depth under Rule #5.

Pro bono is Latin for "for free." Literally it means "for the good."

RECOVERY OF FEES FROM THE CLIENT

The ABA Model Code also takes an affirmative stand on "fee fights" often seen in the 1990s. Based on a 1943 ABA Opinion (No. 250),[3] the ABA's Model Code EC 2-23 says that an attorney "should be zealous in his efforts to avoid controversies over fees with clients." Further, "[h]e should not sue a client for a fee unless necessary to prevent fraud or gross imposition by the client."

In the 1980s, however, the ABA's standards on "gross imposition" slackened. In reality, very few attorneys will ignore the unpaid client bill for the sake of Canon 2. In fact, many law firms employ paralegals to handle the collection of delinquent bills for the firm. The Model Rules' Comment on this subject reads only:

> [I]f a procedure has been established for resolution of fee disputes, such as an arbitration or mediation procedure established by the bar, the lawyer should conscientiously consider submitting to it.[4]

> If you think that $625 million was bad, the fee in the Florida tobacco cases was $2.8 **billion.** The lawyers went to court to fight for their fee. In his decision against the lawyers, the Florida judge estimated that the fees amounted to $7,716 an hour for each of the 12 private attorneys billing 24 hours a day for the 42 months that the case went on. "Perhaps tens of millions or hundreds of millions of dollars might be reasonable," Cohen wrote, "but 2.8 billion dollars simply shocks the conscience of the court." What do you think? Does it shock your conscience? Is it fair?

> To research the law on recoverability of nonlawyer fees in your state, try West's Digest Topic "Costs," key numbers 194 and 207.
>
> For recovery of attorney's fees, see West's Digest Topic "Costs," key number 173(1).

California and other states mandate fee arbitration. California's Business & Professions Code §§ 6200–6206 require that the lawyer give notice to the client of the client's right to elect to arbitrate any fee dispute. This is true in New York, as well. Can you find it in the law?

To recover the fee, of course, the attorney must show that the client retained him or her and that the services performed were with the client's informed consent. A thorough explanation of the fees before beginning the representation and an honest discussion about the anticipated costs will go a long way in avoiding fee disputes. Anyone involved in collecting fees from clients should also be aware that the Fair Debt Collection Practices Act[5] applies to your activities. Last, you need to review the rules on conflicts of interest and collecting fees from clients. Once the law firm sues the client for fees, the law firm is in an adverse position to the client and cannot continue representation.

RECOVERY OF FEES FROM THE OTHER SIDE IN LITIGATION

prevailing means winning

A *prevailing* party may recover attorneys' fees from the other party in only limited circumstances: where attorneys' fees are provided for in a statute and where they are provided for in the contract. This is called the American Rule of attorneys' fees.[6] For example, at the conclusion of the lawsuit, the prevailing party can ask the court to award attorneys' fees under the Federal Rehabilitation Act[7] because the statute specifically provides that in cases of discrimination against individuals with disabilities, the prevailing party is entitled to "reasonable attorneys' fees."[8] The prevailing party prepares a memorandum or declaration setting forth all of the time spent, hourly billing rates, tasks, and costs of the litigation. Ordinarily a separate motion will be heard on the issue of the reasonableness of the fees requested.

Interestingly, statutes and contracts provide for "attorneys' fees." Taken literally, that would mean that other legal professionals would not be included, that the cost of having such an assistant must be "overhead" and taken into account in determining the attorneys' hourly rates. The interpretation of the term "attorneys' fees" has been as far as the United States Supreme Court.

Missouri v. Jenkins[9] was a major school desegregation case in Kansas City, Missouri. The second issue tackled by the United States Supreme Court was "should the fee award compensate the work of paralegals and law clerks by applying the market rate for their work?" The Court:

> Clearly, a "reasonable attorney's fee" under [42 USC § 1988] cannot have meant to compensate only work performed personally by members of the bar. Rather, the term must refer to a reasonable fee for the work product of an attorney . . . [including] . . . secretaries, messengers, librarians, janitors and others whose labor contributes to the work product for which an attorney bills her client; and it must also take into account of other expenses and profit. (at 285)

The Court's footnote ten on page 288 points out: "Of course, purely clerical or secretarial tasks should not be billed at a paralegal rate regardless of who performs them."[10]

In spite of what appears to be a clear message from the Supreme Court, the issue is still far from settled among the state courts. The only way to know for sure is to research your state's law.

From *Multi-Moto v. ITT Commercial Finance,* 806 S.W.2d 560 (Tex.App. 1990), here's a list of things you'll need if you're going to apply to the court for paralegal fees.

> A party may separately assess and include in the award of attorneys' fees compensation for a legal assistant's work, if that assistant performs work traditionally done by an attorney. In order to recover such amounts, the evidence must establish: (1) the qualifications of the legal assistant to perform substantive legal work; (2) that the legal assistant performed substantive legal work under the direction and supervision of an attorney; (3) the nature of the legal work performed; (4) the legal assistant's hourly rate; and (5) the number of hours expended by the legal assistant.

Whenever applying for fees, these factors are essential for any declaration or motion filed with the court. Don't worry about this case being from Texas. This is a good list.

There are cases where the court has reduced the amount of attorney's fees requested because the attorney was performing tasks more properly performed by a paralegal.[11] For the most part, the courts agree that it is the task, not the title of the billing employee, which is determinative of recoverability. Clerical tasks are not billable and will not be recoverable. Tasks that are nonclerical are billable and are usually recoverable at an hourly rate that is appropriate for the task.

REFERRAL FEES

Here's the bottom line: no matter what state you live or work in, you cannot take a referral fee from a lawyer. This is because the ABA and most states agree that a referral fee looks like "buying a claim." Yes, of course, people get paid for their work on a case. Even freelancers or contract lawyers and paralegals get paid. But they may not be paid any more than the responsibility assumed or work performed is worth.

If this is the law, why is it that we hear so much about attorneys and nonattorneys alike being paid referral fees? What is a referral fee and when is it permissible? The ABA Code and Rules apparently disapprove of referral fees by virtue of the absence of a reference approving them. Comment 4, Model Rule 1.5, says:

> A division of fee is a single billing to a client covering the fee of two or more lawyers who are not in the same firm. A division of fee facilitates association of more than one lawyer in a matter in which neither alone could serve the client as well, and most often is used when the fee is contingent and the division is between a referring lawyer and a trial specialist.

In other words, the lawyers who do the work or assume responsibility for the case should get paid accordingly. But this is not a "referral fee" in the traditional sense. A referral fee is a fee paid for doing nothing other than bringing the client to the lawyer. It is *champerty*—the purchasing of a claim or a client.

Champerty is a word that came to us from ancient France. Champertie meant the amount of the crop paid to the lord by way of rent.

In California, referral fees to other lawyers are allowed under the Rules of Professional Conduct only so long as the client has consented in writing, the total fee charged to the client is not increased, and the money is a "gift" for making a recommendation that later results in employment. It cannot be a fee or a reward, and it cannot be made with the understanding that more such "gifts" will be made in the future for future referrals. The rationale in California is this: we don't want lawyers taking cases they are not qualified to take. We want them to refer, for example, criminal defense cases to criminal defense lawyers. But lawyers need to make money just as does everyone else. The state believes that if we let the lawyer make some amount of money instead of nothing from referring the case to a more skilled lawyer, it is more likely to happen. The public is better served that way. Referral fees are only from one lawyer to another. Paralegals cannot accept referral fees. This concept overlaps with improper division of fees covered in Rule #7.

WHAT DO YOU THINK?

You are sent to Japan on a case for Client X. On the very long plane ride to Japan, you work on some other matters for Client M. Should you bill the time you spend on the plane twice, once to Client X and another time to Client M?

CLIENT FILES AND FEES

Repeat after me: "Client files belong to the client."[12] Client files belong to the client. They cannot be "held hostage" to insure the payment of legal fees.[13] This is true even if the contractual agreement between the law firm and the client specifically says that the law firm is entitled to a **retaining lien** on the files.

Several cases have discussed the common law **retaining lien,** or the idea that the attorney has an equitable right to assert a lien that attaches to all papers, money, and other property of the client that the attorney has in his or her possession in order to secure payment of legal fees. Most courts have rejected the common law retaining lien theory in favor of a more important goal of not prejudicing the client's case.[14] Even though the law seems very clear that the client's files must be turned over, in reality, many lawyers still try to hold the files hostage until the client pays the fees.

WHAT DO YOU THINK?

Does absolutely EVERYTHING in the file belong to the client? What about secret attorney thoughts? What about notes about impressions or unprovable facts. Give it some thought. Look up this case for some recent guidance: *Swift, Currie, McGhee & Hiers v. Henry,* 276 Ga. 571 (Ga. May 19, 2003).

A retaining lien is not the same as a **charging lien.** A charging lien secures the legal fees by attaching a lien to a future judgment or settlement in the case. For instance, if a law firm is hired on a contingency fee basis and does work for the client and then the client discharges that firm and hires a second firm, the first firm may file a charging lien in the lawsuit. When the case is settled or a judgment is rendered by the court, the first law firm has a lien on the amount awarded to the client. There may well be a fight about how much the first law firm is entitled to, but money should not be disbursed to the client or the second law firm before the percentages are all decided upon.[15]

> **Model Rule 1.16** Upon termination of representation, a lawyer shall take steps to the extent reasonably practicable to protect a client's interests, such as giving reasonable notice to the client, allowing time for employment of other counsel, surrendering documents and property to which the client is entitled and refunding any advance payment of a fee that has not been earned. Upon the client's request, the lawyer shall provide the client with all of the client's documents, and all documents reflecting work performed for the client.

> Rule 3-700(D)(1) of the California State Bar Rules of Professional Conduct requires that once an attorney's representation has been terminated, the attorney *shall* promptly release to the client all the client's papers and property. "Client papers and property" includes correspondence, pleadings, deposition transcripts, exhibits, physical evidence, expert's reports and other items reasonably necessary to the client's representation."

> Cases on liens can be found in West's Digest Topic "Attorney & Client," key numbers 171 through 190. What's the law in your state?

RULE #4 WRAP-UP

The overriding consideration in client billing is that the fee must be objectively fair. Profit margin on employees is not the barometer to use in determining fairness, but the sophistication and relative bargaining power of the attorney and client are proper considerations. The requirement that the fee be reasonable will override the terms of the contract in appropriate cases. Again, the more you can prove that the client understood the terms of the agreement, the more likely it will be that the agreement will be found to be fair.

RULE #4 REVIEW QUESTIONS

1. What is a billable task? Give some examples of billable and nonbillable tasks.
2. Why should fee agreements with the client be in writing?
3. What is the rationale behind the rule prohibiting paralegals from negotiating fee agreements with clients?

Check list for keeping your time records:

(1) Keep your time records contemporaneously.

(2) Keep accurate and detailed time records.

(3) Keep honest time records.

4. What is a contingency fee agreement? When is a contingency fee agreement used?

5. Define "value billing" and "fixed fee billing." How are they different? How are they the same?

6. What are the different kinds of retainer agreements? Are some more fair than others? Why or why not?

7. Can paralegal hourly fees be recovered from the losing side in litigation? How would you go about convincing a court that your client is entitled to recovery of those fees?

8. What is a referral fee? Can you accept a referral fee?

9. Define the word "champerty." How is it used today? Why is champerty bad?

10. What is a retaining lien? A charging lien? How are they different?

[1] See NALA Model Standards, and *Louisiana Bar v. Edwins,* 540 So.2d 294 (La. 1989).

[2] For an interesting case on this issue, see *Ramirez v. Sturdevant* 21 Cal.App.4th 904, 26 Cal.Rptr.2d 554 (1994), where the California court discussed the problem of the conflict of interest that arises between the client and attorney when the attorney negotiates his own fees as part of the settlement of the client's case against the defendant.

[3] "Ours is a learned profession, not a mere money-getting trade. . . . Suits to collect fees should be avoided. Only where the circumstances imperatively require should resort be had to a suit to compel payment." ABA Opinion No. 250 (1943).

[4] Comment to ABA Model Rules of Professional Conduct, Rule 1.5.

[5] 15 USC Section 1692 et.seq.

[6] In England (the English Rule), the prevailing party always gets fees from the other side.

[7] 29 USC § 794 et seq.

[8] Query whether this means a "reasonable attorney" or a "reasonable fee."

[9] 491 U.S. 274 (1989).

[10] See also footnote seven of the Court's opinion for a rundown on the various federal courts' handling of paralegal time. See also *Landals v. George A. Rolfes Co.,* 454 N.W.2d 891 (Iowa 1990), allowing paralegal fees in an age discrimination case, citing *Missouri v. Jenkins.*

[11] *Smith v. Roher,* 1997 U.S. Dist. Lexis 1411 (1997).

[12] *Matter of Gemmer,* 566 N.E.2d 528 (Ind. 1991).

[13] *Academy of Cal. Optometrists, Inc. v. Sup. Ct.,* 51 Cal.App.3d 999, 124 Cal.Rptr. 668 (1975).

[14] *Home Savings of America v. Malart,* 632 A.2d 827 (N.J.Super. 1993). But see *Matter of Estate of Benney,* 790 P.2d 319 (Colo. 1990) where the Colorado Supreme Court seems to say that Colorado's retaining lien statute is valid. If, for example, the lawyer has been hired to draft a will, in some states the lawyer may be able to keep the will and the notes, research, etc., until the client has paid. See also *In re Century Cleaning Services, Inc.,* 202 B.R. 149 (Bkrtcy.D.Or. 1996).

[15] See *Rhodes v. Martinez,* 925 P.2d 1201 (N.M.App. 1996). For a case where the law firm was entitled to a charging lien, see *Kiernan v. Kiernan,* 649 N.Y.S.2d 612 (1996).

MAKE LEGAL
SERVICES AVAILABLE

ACCESS TO JUSTICE

There is a gap between the need for legal assistance and the satisfaction of that need. This gap is getting larger and larger. The primary reason for this problem is the cost, real or perceived, of legal services. The secondary reason is that many people are unaware of their rights under the law, so they don't see that they have a need for legal assistance. The law appears complex and frightening to most people. There is a perception that only the rich are entitled to justice. Lawyers, even those portrayed on television, do not appear to be honest or caring. As a result, the uneducated and the poor are those who are the least likely to receive legal help, although it is these people who need help the most. This is why there is an affirmative duty placed on all of us to provide better access to the judicial system. We call it access to justice.

Access to justice includes informing people about their legal rights, showing them how the law can help them, and making legal services affordable . . . even if affordable means free.

To see how one state is helping meet the need, see Kentucky's Access to Justice Foundation at *http://www.accesstojustice.org*.

INFORMATION

Our justice system is based on ensuring that people understand their legal rights. The constitution guarantees us the right to a lawyer in criminal matters charged against us, and *Miranda v. Arizona*[1] makes it mandatory that we be informed of that right (as not many of us have the Constitution memorized.) Our other legal rights are not necessarily obvious to us; for example, a public school education for our children might be obvious, but how many of us know that we have a legal right to that education? And there are many legal issues to which we do not have a right but would make life so much easier for us and for our loved ones. An example of this is a will. There is no constitutional guarantee to a will, but with just a little bit of assistance, we can all have a will and our heirs will be thankful that we have one. Because the legal solutions to problems are not always obvious, Model Rule 6.1 and Ethical Consideration 2-2 say that members of the legal profession should assist people in recognizing their legal problems. One way of doing this is to participate in educational programs for laypeople. Another way of assisting people in recognizing their legal problems is advertising.

WHAT DO YOU THINK?

Should everyone have access to legal representation for noncriminal defense matters? Should the government provide representation just as it provides education?

Advertising

Some form of "advertising," that is, letting the public know the attorney's name, telephone number, and address, has always been permitted. If this were not true, members of the public would not be able to find a lawyer when they needed one. Before the 1980s, however, the legal profession was very strict about the kind of advertising that was allowed. The law did not allow attorneys to advertise on television, for example. It did not allow billboards or using the side of a municipal bus as an ad. However, *Bates v. Arizona* changed the laws prohibiting lawyers from advertising more than just their names and whereabouts. Now, since *Bates,* attorneys advertise all over the place, use paid actors, scripts, and explanations about the legal services offered and even invite people to think about a simple headache as a cause of action against employers.

Although the Supreme Court's decision in *Bates* should have ended the controversy about attorney advertising, it did not. In 1984, Attorney Zauderer was publicly reprimanded by the Ohio Supreme Court after running an advertisement entitled "Did You Use This IUD?" which depicted a larger-than-life Dalkon Shield. The ad ran in thirty-six Ohio

---

Bates v. Arizona, 433 U.S. 350, 97 S.Ct. 2691 (1977). The United States Supreme Court held that prohibiting advertising by attorneys was a violation of their First Amendment right to free speech. The Court ruled that because the speech can be regulated by the integrated bar and because such advertising serves to reduce the cost of legal services to the public, it benefits the administration of justice. The advertising in question was a newspaper advertisement that announced the legal work and prices of a legal clinic. It was not improper because it could not be classified as "in-person solicitation."

> In a concurring and dissenting opinion in *Bates,* Chief Justice Burger wrote: **"To be sure, the public needs information concerning attorneys, their work, and their fees. At the same time, the public needs protection from the unscrupulous or the incompetent practitioner anxious to prey on the uninformed."** What do you think about his warning? Has his fear come true?

newspapers. It mentioned that the shield had led to infertility and abortions and invited readers to telephone Zauderer with regard to his representation in a class action against the manufacturer and other parties. The United States Supreme Court reviewed the restrictions on lawyer advertising in *Zauderer v. Disciplinary Counsel.*[2] Zauderer's defense argued that the Ohio regulation violates his First Amendment right to free speech, an argument which may be worth trying in those states that prohibit legal assistant advertising. The Supreme Court upheld the reprimand on the basis that the advertisement was misleading, but affirmed the attorney's right to advertise in what many 1980s legal professionals thought was a less-than-tasteful manner. Even the Supreme Court cannot regulate good taste.

Advertising and the Paralegal

Paralegals and other nonlawyers cannot give legal advice or otherwise deliver legal services directly to the public. For that reason, nonlawyers cannot advertise their services directly to the public such as taking out a page in the telephone directory. However, nonlawyers may advertise their services to attorneys and law firms through letters, advertisements in legal directories, and legal periodical publications. Paralegals and other nonlawyers may be listed with the other legal professionals of firms in the Martindale Hubbell directory.

The Martindale Hubbell directory is a very large listing of law firms and lawyers. You can find it in your law library and at *http://www.martindale.com.*

Of course, paralegals have business cards, which are a sort of advertising. Paralegal business cards must not be deceptive in any way. For example, it is wise not to include the designation "notary" on your business card with your "paralegal" designation. This is because some cultures and languages associate "notario" with a person who can practice law.

There are some cases of paralegals practicing law without a license (see Rule #7 UPL) and using deceptive business cards. In one case, where the paralegal argued that his business card was covered by his First Amendment right to commercial speech, the South Carolina court ruled that deceptive or false speech is not protected by the First Amendment, and the words "If your civil rights have been violated—call me" were unlawful because they were deceptive.[3] Such words would lead the average person to believe that he was licensed to practice law.

Solicitation

Although advertising is now permitted, solicitation is not. The ABA Model Rules prohibit in-person "soliciting":

> A lawyer may not solicit professional employment from a prospective client with whom the lawyer has no family or prior professional relationship, by mail, in person or otherwise, when a significant motive for the lawyer's doing so is the lawyer's pecuniary gain. The term "solicit" includes contact in person, by telephone or telegraph, by letter or other writing, or by other communication directed to a specific recipient, but does not include letters addressed or advertising circulars distributed generally. . . . (Rule 7.3 Direct Contact with Prospective Clients)

Simply put, the difference between solicitation and advertising is that solicitation is in person, by telephone, or by written communication that is directed to a specific individual. Advertising, on the other hand, is directed to the public at large.

Attorneys cannot solicit individuals as clients and cannot allow their employees to solicit them. The lawyers you see portrayed on television, hanging out in hospitals and mortuaries, trolling for clients, are fictional.

In *Idaho State Bar v. Jenkins*,[4] the court discussed the incidents involving contact of prospective clients by Paralegal Landeros for the purpose of soliciting them for her employer. In one case, Landeros contacted the parents of a young man who had been killed in an automobile accident. She went to their home and told the Martinez family that Jenkins "was the best lawyer in the firm" and that he had sent her out to their home to see what she could do "to help the family." Holding that it was not the attorney's fault that the paralegal was engaging in unlawful in-person solicitation, the court said:

> While one might characterize Francis Landeros as a loose cannon rolling around the deck of Jenkins' law office, the overwhelming evidence established a firm policy, supported by frequent staff

meetings, aimed at educating Mr. Jenkins' non-lawyer staff about impermissible in-person solicitations. This program is precisely the kind of action a lawyer must take to assure himself that the impermissible conduct itself, as well as the consequences of an in-person solicitation, can be avoided or mitigated.

What Paralegal Landeros was doing was clearly solicitation because it was in-person, initiated by her, for the purpose of securing a client for her employer for profit. Note that it was the lawyer who was on the hook for the improper conduct of his employee because there was no penalty that the court could impose on the paralegal. The court has the authority to issue an injunction to prohibit her from similar conduct in the future, but, as there is no regulatory body that licenses or regulates her, no penalty could be imposed on her.

It is not considered improper solicitation to talk to a current or past client about representation in another case.

Good Solicitation

Just as the Supreme Court has determined that advertising can be good for society, it has decided that some in-person solicitation is good for society. For example, in one Supreme Court case, a woman solicited clients for the ACLU to file a case against the state of South Carolina when it was discovered that South Carolina was requiring women to undergo sterilization in order to qualify for Medicaid benefits. The State Bar of South Carolina filed an action against the attorney for unlawful solicitation after she met with some women and wrote them letters offering the free services of the ACLU. On appeal, the Supreme Court found that her actions were not improper writing:

> This was not in-person solicitation for pecuniary gain. Appellant was communicating an offer of free assistance by attorneys associated with the ACLU, not an offer predicated on entitlement to a share of any monetary recovery. And her actions were undertaken to express personal political beliefs and to advance the civil-liberties objectives of the ACLU, rather than to derive financial gain.[5]

> Law Firm Spotlight: Cleary Gottlieb Steen & Hamilton has offices in New York and Washington, DC, in addition to nine cities in foreign countries. In 2003, this firm joined the top ten of The American Lawyer's annual pro bono honor roll of the 200 highest-grossing U.S.-based firms, coming in at #9 and billing 44,361 volunteer hours in 2003. Those numbers put Cleary at #4 on American Lawyer's 2003 "A-list" behind Davis Polk Wardwell, Debevoise Plimpton, and Paul Weiss Rifkind Warton & Garrison.

So, solicitation that is not for personal gain, that informs members of the public of legal rights they might otherwise not have known about, and furthers some civil liberty objective is "good" solicitation.

Corporate Clients

In-person solicitation prohibitions do not apply to corporate clients, however. For example, there is no law that says you cannot take the president of the bank out to lunch and ask her or him to use your law firm's services. The solicitation rules are designed to protect the unsophisticated user of legal services, not companies.

WHAT DO YOU THINK?

Robin Ficker, an attorney, gets a list of people who have been issued traffic tickets. He writes letters to those people who could do jail time as a penalty and offers to represent them in court. The letter is addressed to each individual, recites the traffic offense, and all possible penalties. Is this solicitation or direct mail advertising? To help you with your answer, look at *Ficker v. Curran,* (1996) 950 F. Supp. 123, affirmed 119 F.3d 1150.

Technology

Some states have specifically opined that lawyers and their paralegal employees cannot solicit clients via the Internet. For example, Florida, West Virginia, Virginia, Michigan, and Utah all have rules prohibiting solicitation of clients through Internet chat rooms. Chat rooms are defined as "real-time communications between computer users."[6]

However, Web sites as a form of advertising have generally been found harmless, so long as they do not include false or deceptive information. Because Web sites are advertising, they will have to conform to the regulations of the law firm's state regarding advertising.[7] Some states require a hard copy of the home page to be on file with the regulating agency[8] or have a copy of the entire Web site in some retrievable format.[9]

Law Firm Spotlight: 2004 *American Lawyer Magazine's* Best Law Firm to work for—Debevoise Plimpton (New York) with a score of 197 out of a possible 200 for pro bono work. Heller Ehrman White & McAuliffe (San Francisco) came in second. You can find these firms online at *http://www.debevoise.com* and *http://www.hewm.com*.

Direct Mail

Somewhere between traditional advertising and solicitation is direct mail. Sometimes referred to as "direct mail advertising," sometimes "direct mail solicitation," direct mail is legal.[10] Direct mail is often used in mass disaster cases and in many types of legal matters where a list of prospective clients can be obtained. For instance, many courts make the list of upcoming residential foreclosures available. A law firm gets a copy of this list from the court and sends out a mass mailing to everyone on the list touting that firm's ability to relieve the homeowner from the foreclosure.

WHAT DO YOU THINK?

Should a Web site have to comply with the advertising requirements of *EVERY* state (because the Web site touches every state) or just the states where the law firm has offices?

Whereas advertising to the general public is permitted because it is subject to scrutiny by the public, these direct and private communications to a prospective client are not subject to the same kind of review. The fear that these private statements are misleading is balanced against the public's need to be informed about legal services and the attorney's right to free speech. By keeping the communications public, the ABA hopes to satisfy the public's need and the attorneys' rights while regulating the truth and accuracy of the advertising.

Paralegals, or those who pretend to be paralegals, do not have the legal right to advertise or use direct mail advertising to the general public.[11] This is because to advertise paralegal services to the public would be to offer to practice law without a license. In one such case in Illinois, a "paralegal" company called National Legal Professional Associates,[12] used direct mail to contact prison inmates with the intent of convincing them to use their services in addition to their criminal defense attorney.[13] The marketing campaign was designed to convince inmates that their lawyers were not looking out for their best interests or were, perhaps, incompetent and lazy. The effect of the marketing was that inmates began to respect the advice of NLPA over that of their attorneys, effectively turning the attorney-paralegal relationship on its head. One judge took exception to this practice and issued a summons for the owner of NLPA. After finding that the company engaged in the unauthorized practice of law, he ordered the disgorgement of all fees paid and restitution made to the families of inmates who had wasted their money on NLPA's services. An injunction was issued restricting NLPA's activities. The judge made particular note of NLPA's "unsolicited marketing activities."

In-person solicitation is still improper, whether by an attorney or nonattorney. The line between solicitation and helping a member of the public understand a legal problem is not a clear one, but the motivation of the legal professional is a guide: If the in-person communication is motivated by the desire to make money, it is probably improper solicitation. If it is motivated by a desire to assist a member of the public in recognizing a legal problem, it is more likely proper.

WHAT DO YOU THINK?

Is direct mail advertising more like solicitation or more like advertising? Should it be allowed?

Mass Disasters

Several states have enacted statutes that prohibit any contact for a certain amount of time with people who have been charged with crimes or people who are related to victims of mass disasters. These statutes are designed to protect people from making choices about legal representation while they are especially vulnerable. Although these statutes have been challenged, they have been upheld.

Paralegals are held to the same regulations as an attorney with regard to solicitation of clients. In discussions with laypeople, it is important to be aware of allowing the layperson to lead the discussion. In other words, the layperson should ask the legal professional (attorney or nonattorney) for a referral to an attorney or firm before the referral is offered. In the ordinary conversation between friends, this isn't an issue. It becomes a legal/ethical issue when, for example, you hand your business card to a person who has just been injured in a car accident.

Most state professional responsibility rules and codes require the legal professional to refrain from actively seeking out people who may have

---

In *Florida Bar v. Went For It, Inc.,* 515 U.S. 619 (1995), the Supreme Court upheld a statute banning contact with victims and families of victims of mass disasters for thirty days. Notice the name of the defendant in the case. Where do you think the name came from?

In April 1994, Lawrence Canter and wife, Martha Siegel (the law firm of Canter & Siegel), sent a posting to over 6,000 "Usenet" newsgroups. The message offered the law firm's services to anyone who wanted to take part in a U.S. government lottery of "green card" work permits. The subject line was: "Green Card Lottery 1994 May be the Last One!! Sign up now!!" As many as 6 million people may have received the message. What do you think? Good advertising? Direct e-mail? Solicitation? Or spam?

legal claims and to refrain from "convincing" laypeople that they do have a legal claim. The problem that arises, of course, is that laypeople may be irreparably injured if they do not seek legal assistance to pursue their claims or refuse to believe they have a claim. The ethical course is to let them make their own decision and refer them to a lawyer if they ask for assistance and you are not a lawyer. Lawsuits are costly, time consuming, and often very upsetting. Many people will choose not to pursue a legal claim for reasons known only to themselves.

If the purpose of prohibiting in-person solicitation is the presumed inability of the client to say "no," should the rule be applicable to Internet chat room interaction? Why or why not?

RULE #5 WRAP-UP

Access to the judicial system for all Americans is a lofty goal. It is a goal we aspire to and we work toward. Bringing information to people who have legal claims but may not know their rights is part of making legal services available. Even though some advertising is distasteful to us (and recognizing that taste is a difficult if not impossible thing to legislate), advertising is a good thing. It makes it easier for members of the public to find help in legal matters. So, advertising can be both good and bad. Solicitation can also be good and bad. In-person contact for the purpose of getting a paying client may fall under the rules of prohibited solicitation. Informing members of the public of their rights and encouraging them to "sign on" may also be a good thing, such as in the case of *Primus* and the ACLU litigation to end the practice of sterilizing women. Direct mail falls somewhere in between advertising and solicitation. It, too, can be used for good and for those up to no good.

The Internet has posed some new questions in the world of advertising and solicitation, as have mass disasters. In the final analysis, what we're looking for is informing the public, helping the public gain access to the judicial system when it is needed, and not abusing the First Amendment right to commercial speech.

RULE #5 REVIEW QUESTIONS

1. Is it your duty to give information to the public? Why or why not? In what circumstances would it be improper for you to give information to the public?

2. What is the definition of "advertising"? When did advertising legal services on television become legal?

3. What is "direct mail advertising"? How is it different from plain advertising?

4. What is "solicitation"? When is it good? When is it prohibited?

5. What are Internet "chat rooms"? Why might they be a dangerous place for a lawyer or paralegal?

6. What was the point of the case *Florida Bar v. Went For It, Inc.?* What was the defendants' argument?

7. Freedom of speech stems from our Constitution. Do you know where it is in the Constitution? What other freedoms might concern paralegals?

8. Visit some law firm Internet sites. What do they have in common? How are they different from each other?

9. What are some things paralegals can do to help the cause of access to justice?

10. Visit *http://www.martindale.com.* What is there? What is the purpose of the Web site?

---

[1] 384 U.S. 436, 86 S. Ct. 1602 (1966).

[2] 105 S.Ct. 2265 (1985).

[3] *South Carolina v. Robinson,* 468 S.E.2d 290 (1996).

[4] 816 P.2d 335 (Idaho 1991).

[5] *In re Primus,* 438 U.S. 432 (1978).

[6] Florida advisory opinion A-00-1 (8/15/2000): An attorney may not solicit prospective clients through Internet chat rooms, defined as real-time communications between computer users. For guidance on the issue, the Florida panel looked at opinions from other states and relied upon four in particular: West Virginia L.E.I. 98-03 (10/16/98), Michigan Opinion RI-276 (7/11/96), Utah 97-10 (10/24/97), and Virginia A-0110 (04/14/98).

[7] Iowa Ethics Op. 96-1 (1996); Pennsylvania Ethics Op. 96-17 (1996); South Carolina Ethics Op. 94-27 (1995); and Tennessee Ethics Op. 95-A-570 (1995).

[8] See, for example, Florida's Fla. Bar Standing Comm. on Adver. Internet Guidelines, at 2. If the home page contains no audio, photographs, illustrations, or other information other than as outlined in Rule 4.7, 2(n)(1)-(10) the home page need not be filed for review.

[9] See, for example, Arizona's Comm. on Rules of Professional Conduct of Ariz., Op. No. 97-04 dated April 7, 1997.

[10] *Shapero v. Kentucky Bar Association,* 486 U.S. 466, 475 (1988).

[11] There is an exception in California for Legal Document Assistants. See California Business & Professions Code Sections 6400 through 6415.

[12] NLPA was based in Ohio. The federal court had jurisdiction over NLPA because it was practicing law in Illinois.

[13] *U.S. v. Johnson* (7th Cir. 2003).

REPRESENT EACH CLIENT WITH ZEAL AND DEDICATION . . . WITHIN THE BOUNDS OF THE LAW

DUE PROCESS AS OUR CORNERSTONE

At the foundation of our American system of justice is the concept of "due process." Exactly how much process is due depends in large part on the circumstances. The 6th Amendment of our Constitution guarantees us the right to counsel when we are charged in a criminal matter. And no doubt we are all familiar with "the *Miranda* warning" given to the accused: you have the right to an attorney and if you cannot afford one, one will be appointed to you. And we've heard the part about "you have the right to remain silent" from the 5th Amendment. But the Bill of Rights guarantees the criminal accused more than that: not to be deprived of life, liberty, or property without **due process of law.** And the 6th Amendment guarantees us an impartial jury of our peers in a speedy and public trial, to be confronted with witnesses, and the right to subpoena witnesses. We are protected against excessive bail under the 8th Amendment. All of these things are part of the process we are due because we are in America.

Due Process Requirements to the Client

The key word is "zeal." Zeal means enthusiastic devotion to a cause, ideal, or goal, and tireless diligence in its furtherance. A synonym would be passion.

In examining these rights under the microscope of the United States Supreme Court, we are reminded again and again that we have the right to the representation of an attorney at every step in the proceedings.[1] And where the attorney's representation is lacking in quality, care, and diligence, the constitutional guarantee of due process is violated.[2] So it's not just an attorney we're guaranteed when accused of a criminal matter—it's a competent, loyal, and zealous attorney. Outside of the criminal justice system context, when we hire an attorney in a civil matter or to simply draft a will, we are entitled to a competent and loyal attorney who will represent us zealously.

Due Process Requirements to the System

But balanced against the attorney's duties to his or her client of competence, loyalty, and zealousness, is the attorney's (and paralegal's) duties to "the system of justice." In other words, the system cannot work unless the professionals in the system have respect for the system; unless they deal with the system with honesty and integrity; unless they zealously do their job "within the bounds of the law."

WHERE IS THE BOUNDARY OF THE LAW?

The "bounds of the law" in many cases will be hard to determine. The rules of professional conduct are broad, are difficult to apply, and change continually. ABA Model Code EC 7-3 says that where the line between the lawful and the unlawful is difficult to find, we should look to whether they are in the role of an "adviser" or an "advocate." This makes sense. Advocates, such as when the lawyer represents the client in a criminal matter, must take the facts as they find them. They may interpret the facts but must not try to change them in their own or their client's mind. They should, however, interpret factual situations in their client's favor while working as advocates. Advisors need to view the facts one way, and then another way, and perhaps a third and fourth way in order to give the client all of the possible alternatives.

ABA Model Rule 2.1 says that the bounds of the law may not always be what they seem. In representing the client, we should look not only to what the law says but "to other considerations such as moral, economic, social and political factors."

Frankly, you'll be amazed at some of the things so-called "professionals" do in the zealous representation of their clients. There's a line there between zealous and downright illegal. Let's go find the line.

Suppressing Evidence

We (legal professionals) are specifically prohibited from suppressing (hiding) evidence that we or our clients have a legal obligation to reveal.[3] This prohibition extends to hiding witnesses as well.[4] When we know our client has suppressed evidence or hidden witnesses, we have an obligation to notify the court. When we don't do that, we become responsible for the acts of the client.[5] The reasoning behind these regulations is that the proper administration of justice and due process require that the court be made aware of all evidence and witnesses. Without access to the evidence, it cannot make an educated and just decision.

It is a commonly held (but wrong) belief that the attorney can hide the weapon used by the client in the crime because the weapon is privileged or confidential. This is a wrong belief because these items are not necessarily protected under attorney/client privilege (depending upon the source of the weapon) and not necessarily "confidential information," because it is an instrument of a crime, not information. Let's take some examples.

When your client says: "I stole this rifle from Walmart," the confession is confidential. (If you don't believe that it is, review Rule #2). When the client tells you where the dead bodies of his victims are, that information is confidential.[6] However, if you take physical possession of incriminating evidence, you have an affirmative duty to give the incriminating evidence to the proper authorities.[7] If the incriminating evidence is removed from its location with your assistance, then the details of where the physical item was found, the original condition of the item (plus any testing you've had done) must be disclosed regardless of your duty of loyalty to the client, confidentiality, and the attorney/client privilege.[8] If you, acting in good faith, change the crime scene in any way, you violate the rules that protect the public's interest in effective and fair prosecution. You have a duty to preserve the evidence in the same form as it was. If you change it (for example, wipe fingerprints off of the evidence), the prosecution will be deprived of the opportunity to discover the evidence.

The client's communication to you telling you where the evidence is, however, and your observations made as a consequence of confidential communications are protected from disclosure.

Incriminating evidence that you get through someone other than your client is not protected by the attorney/client privilege or a duty of confidentialiy. You must turn the evidence over to the prosecution, and you may be required to testify about how you came into possession of the evidence.[9] In these situations, the duty of client loyalty gives way to the need of the public to prosecute criminals. In the famous *Belge* case (where the client told his lawyer where to find the dead bodies), photographs of the body taken by the lawyer were also protected and not subject to voluntary disclosure. It is only when the lawyer takes possession of incriminating physical evidence from its present location that the duty of voluntary disclosure arises.[10]

> **WHAT DO YOU THINK?**
>
> You are interviewing a client of your criminal defense law firm. He tells you that he has killed his 4-year-old son, but he has not been arrested for that crime because no one knows that his son is missing. He was arrested on a burglary charge. What should you do?

Not all attorneys hide evidence to protect the client. Sometimes they have their own self-interest in mind. In one case, an attorney for the executor of an estate received a letter from a relative saying that the relative surrendered all interest in the decedent's estate.[11] The attorney concealed the letter from the only remaining interested heir and also told that heir that the estate would be contested by the other relative for some time. The attorney did this, of course, so that his legal fees would continue to grow. The California Supreme Court made a finding that the attorney had hidden the letter for his own gain.

Fabricating Evidence

Instead of hiding evidence, what about making up evidence? Back in the early days of photocopy technology, this wasn't so easy. Technology today, however, makes the duplication of any document an almost easy task. However, if you deliberately fabricate evidence or knowingly allow the client to fabricate evidence for the purpose of putting it before the court, you are guilty of "perpetrating a fraud upon the court" and "obstructing justice."[12] This fabrication can take several forms.

Tampering with Evidence

One of my personal favorites is the case of a defense attorney who enlarged the bullet hole in state's evidence (a leather belt) by forcing a dowel through it, thereby ruining the probative value of the evidence.[13] He was disbarred.

Inducing a Witness to Testify Falsely

*To **suborn** is to induce a person to do an illegal act.*

An attorney will be disbarred for obstruction of justice if found guilty of *subornation of perjury* or otherwise tampering with witnesses. Where the attorney makes an agreement to pay or have the client pay a witness for lying under oath, that attorney will be disbarred.[14] Or how about where the attorney advises his client to lie about the date on which her car accident occurred to avoid a problem with the statute of limitations?[15] Or the attorney who advises his client to "play dumb" and, if questioned about certain past convictions, to deny them.[16] Or paying money to police officers to influence their testimony, whether to induce them to testify truthfully or falsely.[17] An attorney may reimburse witnesses for their expenses but must not pay them more than an amount that reimburses them for loss incidental to having been a witness.[18]

WHAT DO YOU THINK?

If a lawyer offers a lot of money to a witness of facts "if we win," is that inducing that witness to fabricate evidence? Look at *Florida Bar v. Wohl,* 842 So. 2d 811 (Fla. March 20, 2003).

Allowing a Witness to Testify Falsely

Even where the false testimony isn't the lawyer's idea, the lawyer has an obligation not to allow the client to offer false testimony or false documents. Perjured statements by clients are outside of the attorney/client privilege and are not protected.[19] That the client has said he will lie on the witness stand, for example, is protected by the attorney/client privilege. But if he actually does lie on the witness stand, his earlier statement to you will not be protected, and you will have to admit it to a court. Then you, as the legal professional, have violated this rule by allowing the client to follow through with the lie. If the client tells you he intends to commit perjury, the best course of action is to convince the client to only tell the truth. Failing that, the attorney must withdraw from the representation "if that will remedy the situation." If it will not, the attorney should make a disclosure to the court. The ABA Model Rules do not reconcile this action with the duty of confidentiality. Apparently, truthfulness to the court is simply more important than the duty of confidentiality in this limited area.

Affidavits. Obviously, lying to the court in an affidavit is a mistake. Where an attorney filed an affidavit for an extension of time that stated

---

In *Johns v. Smyth,* 176 F. Supp 949 (E.D. Va. 1959), defense counsel did not offer oral testimony nor argue his client's defense before the jury. The attorney later told the court that he had reason to believe that his client's story was untrue and he could not in good conscience argue that it was true. Whereas the court agreed that the attorney could not properly manufacture a defense or "plant the seeds of falsehood" in his client's mind, it could not approve of the attorney's virtual abandonment of an attempt to represent his client simply because the attorney had reason to doubt his client's testimony.

The court acknowledged that it is often difficult to differentiate between the error in judgment of attorneys and their lack of best efforts. Where attorneys would choose for tactical reasons to forego oral argument or to examine their client as a witness, it could not be considered an omission constituting client neglect. In *Johns v. Smyth,* the court did not consider the attorney's acts and omissions as tactical maneuvers, especially in the light of the attorney's later admission that he did not believe in his client's innocence.

that he had the flu and was unable to work and that turned out to be a lie, the attorney was subject to discipline.[20]

Making False Documents

This violates the rule even when the false documents aren't created in the context of representing a client. Where an attorney received loans from a bank via false representation and gave untruthful deposition testimony about the loans, his license to practice law was revoked.[21]

> **WHAT DO YOU THINK?**
>
> The attorney you work for alters a check after it has been cashed and uses a copy of the altered check as an exhibit filed with the court. What will happen to the attorney when his deceit is discovered? To help you in your research, see *Reznick v. State Bar* 460 P.2d 969 (Cal. 1969).

THE PRACTICE OF DECEIT

Being deceitful seems to be an everyday event in some form or another. When practiced within the job, however, the deceit of the legal professional becomes a matter for investigation by the court, the state bar, or other disciplinary authority.

The ABA Model Rule of Professional Conduct 4.1 says: A lawyer, in representing a client, **may not knowingly make a false statement of material fact or of law to a third person.** Model Rule 8.4(c) says that it is professional misconduct to engage in conduct involving dishonesty, fraud, deceit, or misrepresentation.

There are many cases that speak of the "materiality" of the deceit. Cases about legal practitioners deceiving beneficiaries about the amount of their inheritance; lawyers simulating clients' signatures on settlement checks; or stories of lawyers participating in other obvious connivance aimed at the court, opposing counsel, or their own clients litter the reports. All of these are clear examples of "material" deceit. The kind of deceit that has not been discussed at length by the courts is the potentially immaterial deceit. Here's the rule: when determining the materiality of the deceit, look at the task at hand and not the ultimate outcome of the case. In other words, how material was the deception to accomplishing the task? If the deceptive representation was crucial to the accomplishment of the task, it is a "material fact" for purposes of Model Rule 4.1.

As a common example, the task is "find the defendant who is evading service of process." It can be a simple matter to call the defendant's employer, say that you are an old girlfriend of the defendant and would like to look him up. "Could I please have his home address?" The task has been accomplished. The cost was a small lie (presuming, of course, that you are not the defendant's old girlfriend).

In this instance, the lie was told clearly within the "representation of the client." Although the misrepresentation was immaterial to the outcome of the case, it was enormous when analyzed in the context of the task at hand (getting the defendant's address). This is where the average legal professional fails in the analysis. We tend to think of "materiality" as going to some ultimate issue in the case and not to the task at hand.

Deceit in Procedure of Discovery

Over the years, some stories of outrageous deceit have circulated in the legal community. One person who works for a large, well-known firm tells a story of a complex leveraged buyout negotiation process that was going on between his firm and another. An associate of his firm, as the story goes, was told to dress up like a messenger and retrieve a package from opposing counsel. The package was to go to the opposing counsel's client, but before it went, the "messenger" was to make a copy of the documents in order to gain an advantage in the negotiations.

It is not difficult to see that this deceptive practice took place during the representation of a client, albeit in a nonlitigation setting, but during representation nonetheless. Even though the deception might not have affected the ultimate outcome of the representation, the goal was to get a copy of documents belonging to someone else, and the deceptive practice was material in accomplishing that goal.

A more commonplace instance of deceit in the law office has to do with the in-house postage meter. Interrogatory response deadlines come and go, but if the missed deadline is only a day or so old, it is an easy matter to change the date on the postage meter so that it will appear that the envelope was mailed on the correct day. Again, if the task at hand is mailing in a timely fashion under the rules of discovery, changing the date on the envelope is not "material" to the outcome of most cases, but it is a false statement of material fact regarding the mailing.

Another common example of law office deceit is the law office employee who signs the client's name to discovery document *attestation* or has the client presign forms. It does not seem such a horrible thing if the law firm has the client's permission to sign the document in the client's absence for the sake of expediency. Several courts, however, have strongly disagreed with that position. A better idea is to get opposing counsel's agreement to allow the lawyer to sign for the client as "attorney-in-fact" until such time as the client returns and can sign the document or attestation personally. If the other counsel has knowledge and has agreed to it, it should not be a problem explaining the situation to a judge later. It is not a misrepresentation of material fact if the lawyer signs his/her name in place of the client's name.

attestation: An affirmation that the document is true.

Employees and Deceit

Even lawyers who recognize that a deceptive act is improper if they do it commonly believe that they can shield themselves by getting someone else to do it. Model Rule 5.3 (on the supervision of nonlawyer employees) makes it clear that the lawyer is on the hook for all activities of employees that would be a violation of professional ethics if engaged in by a lawyer.

Therefore! The paralegal who is instructed to use deceptive practices to obtain the address of a person to be served with process is guilty, on behalf of the employer, of deceptive practices.

So, what can you do? You want to keep your job. You've been asked to do something illegal such as notarize a presigned document or sign a declaration that is backdated. It is something that the attorney would not do, but thinks it is somehow not improper to ask you to do it. What are your options?

HARASSING JURORS

In the John Grisham book *Run Away Jury,* the antagonists plant a person on the jury (John Cusack) so that he can influence the outcome of the trial. The antagonists, however, weren't working for the other side of the case or the lawyer or client on either side. They had their own motives. For a lawyer to be involved (Dustin Hoffman, plaintiff's counsel, was invited to participate in the jury tampering scam but declined) would have been a serious violation of this rule. Of course, members of a jury can be investigated for possible interest in the outcome of the case, unauthorized communications about the case, or other reasons that would cause the members to be disqualified from serving.[22] These investigations, however, must not be "vexatious or harassing," and any improper conduct by or toward a jury member must be reported to the court promptly.[23]

OVERPAYING EXPERT WITNESSES

The rule has always been that expert witnesses may be paid a "reasonable amount" for their services, but not an "excessive amount." How much is reasonable and where the line is to "excessive" remains an unknown. Certainly in high-profile cases, such as O.J. Simpson's criminal trial, the experts were paid exorbitant fees. Perhaps the status of the witness and the defendant, along with the complexity of the expert issue, are factors in the "excessive" determination. It has also traditionally been the rule that witnesses should not be paid a contingency fee because such an arrangement may influence their testimony. In light of the many times an expert is needed in contingency cases, however, this tradition is being eroded.

WHAT DO YOU THINK?

A lawyer offers to act as a witness in exchange for $500,000. Should he be disciplined? To give you a head start, look up *U.S. v. Blaszak,* 349 F.3d 881 (6th Cir. 2003).

COURTESY TO OPPOSING COUNSEL

This part of the rules of ethics does not come naturally to many people. It is, nevertheless, the rule, and arguably a better way to practice law. Remember this: the client is the litigant, not you. The client may have bad feelings toward the person on the other side of the matter, but you should not. Legal professionals should not allow the client's feelings to influence their attitude toward the opposing counsel.[24] No matter how tough litigation gets, a legal professional must always maintain his or her professionalism. Those who fail to offer the ordinary civilities of litigation, such as continuances, will be sanctioned.[25]

Personal attacks on opposing counsel are not permitted under any circumstances, regardless of what you may have seen on television. A criminal defense attorney was held in direct criminal contempt for making personal attacks against a prosecutor, accusing the prosecutor of "lying and cheating," even though the trial judge had not cautioned or warned counsel that his conduct could result in contempt, because his conduct was facially contemptuous. There were 9 pages of trial transcript that showed repeated personal attacks against the prosecutor such as, "Let's see if we can cheat some more today . . . cheat, cheat, cheat."[26]

Some other specific instances of conduct that have been grounds for disciplinary action include calling opposing counsel "a sneak and a snitch" in open court;[27] accusing opposing counsel of bribing a witness and threatening physical violence;[28] and accusing opposing counsel of "playing dirty pool," using "smear tactics," "sandbagging witnesses," and a myriad of other colloquialisms.[29]

It is important for all legal professionals to maintain composure at all times during communications with opposing counsel and others in the judicial system. Personal attacks, rude comments, snide remarks, or statements made in anger will rarely, if ever, serve to help a situation and will more often than not exacerbate problems. Sometimes being calm can be of invaluable assistance to the people around you.

OTHERWISE BREAKING THE LAW

It is never proper to encourage or aid a client in a violation of the law (Rules 1.2[d] and 3.1). The legal professional as advisor can appropriately counsel a client as to the probable outcome of a course of action (Rule 2.1;

see also EC 7-5). It is also appropriate to continue to represent the client after the client has unilaterally taken action that the legal professional has advised against or knows will not be the most beneficial for the client. It is not appropriate, however, for the legal professional to knowingly assist a client in taking illegal action or making frivolous claims. It is misconduct for the professional to encourage the client to commit a criminal act or to advise the client about how to avoid the consequences of a criminal act.

COMMUNICATION WITH OPPOSING PARTY

Model Rule 4.2 says that the legal professional must not communicate with an opposing party except through that party's counsel. This is because the legal professional who is speaking directly to the opposing party may be seen to be taking an unfair advantage. Of course, opposing counsel may give permission for to speak with the client. In some instances, the attorney who is also a party to the action may speak directly with the other party. The Comments to the Rule suggest that the attorney-party's fundamental rights as a litigant outweigh the state's interest in preventing direct communication with the opposing party. In other states, however, even the attorney who is in pro se may not communicate with the other party if the other party is represented by counsel.[30]

WHAT DO YOU THINK?

You have credible evidence that the defendant corporation is systematically destroying relevant evidence. You want to get information from, at the very least, the corporation's management level employees, director of corporate security, director of human resources, and chief of uniformed security. Can you have ex parte communications with these people? To aid you in your answer, read *Cronin v. Eighth Judicial District Court,* 781 P.2d 1150 (1989).

Model Rule 4.3 warns the legal professional not to allow an opposing party who is not represented by counsel to believe that the legal professional is disinterested. Often, the Comment says, unrepresented people assume that a lawyer is simply a disinterested authority on the law. The lawyer should correct that misunderstanding and should not give any legal advice to the unrepresented person other than the advice to obtain legal representation. These rules have few exceptions. The best course for legal professionals is to not communicate with any party to an action who may have a conflicting interest except through that party's attorney. If the party does not have counsel, explain that your job is only to do the best for your client, not to help the adverse party, and that the unrepresented person should seek the assistance of counsel. It is not the unauthorized practice of law to advise an unrepresented person to obtain counsel. Further, it would not be considered giving the opposing party legal advice to suggest some places where that person may be assisted at no cost, such as referring the unrepresented person to a free legal clinic.

COURTESY TO THE COURT

It seems obvious that it is improper to engage in conduct intended to disrupt the court (Model Rule 3.5[c]). The advocate is supposed to stand firm against abuse by a judge but should not reciprocate, in the manner of two wrongs not making a right, and the fact that the judge has the power of contempt and the lawyer does not. The best thing the lawyer can do is protect the record for review by a higher court and refrain from belligerence or theatrics.

GIVE THE COURT ONLY TRUTHFUL STATEMENTS

In addition to courtesy, complete honesty is also a must for the legal professional. Model Rule 3.3 treats this duty of candor toward the tribunal. It is improper to make a false statement of fact or law to a tribunal. For example, if a lawyer asks for a continuance for his subpoenaed witness to arrive at the court, and the court later finds out that the witness had not been subpoenaed, the lawyer will land in contempt of court.

Model Rule 3.3(c) offers one of the most striking questions ever discussed in a classroom setting or strategic trial meeting: What do I do if the client tells me that he's going to commit perjury? The Rule says that the lawyer may refuse to offer evidence that the lawyer reasonably believes is false. The conflict between the legal professional's duty to the client and duty to the public is almost overwhelming. Is there one answer? Does it matter if your client's case is civil or criminal?

In *McCann v. Municipal Court,* 270 Cal.Rptr. 640 (Cal. 1990), the defense attorney was held in direct contempt (contemptuous on the face of the statement) for making the following comments to the municipal court judge: "I will not move on." "I will not move on in this issue until you haul me away." "You're not going to convict my client." "You're not my mother." "If you're going to convict my client, I'm going to react."

GIVE THE COURT ALL OF THE LAW

Probably the most overlooked duty is our duty to disclose law that is contrary to our client's position when that law is not disclosed by opposing counsel. Does that mean that we have to do our opponent's job? Yes, that's exactly what Model Rule 3.3(a)(4) requires. And the Rule is substantially identical to DR 7-102(A)(3), so this not new law. If we know of controlling law that is directly opposed to our position, the best tactic is to cite it for the court, be up-front, and distinguish it on its facts or another way. Trying to hide the *controlling law* is never a good ploy.

*Controlling law is the law that **controls** the outcome, so it is in effect on that issue at the present time.*

LYING TO THE COURT AND DICTA

Rule 3.1 Comment 1 says that legal professionals can urge any permissible construction of the law in representing the client. Law schools and paralegal training institutions spend a great deal of time discussing "dicta," or that part of a judicial decision or opinion that is not directly related to the holding of the court. Many instructors admonish that it is wholly improper to use a dictum, to cite from it or quote it. In practice, however, this is not the case. A more realistic rule is that dicta are entitled to consideration as being a persuasive authority, but they are not binding as authority within the meaning of *stare decisis*.

Stare decisis is a Latin phrase. It is the doctrine under which courts adhere to precedent on questions of law in order to insure certainty, consistency, and stability in the administration of justice.

It is conceivable that a dictum that is repeated by the courts over a period of time becomes precedent as strong and persuasive as a rule of law. Further, some courts have held that dicta may be entitled to persuasive consideration because of the prestige of the judge who wrote them,[31] and dicta of the United States Supreme Court should be considered very persuasive.[32]

It is certainly permissible to use dicta when drafting a legal brief or other persuasive document. It should be cited or quoted, however, in a fashion that is appropriate and not misleading. It is also inadvisable to cite a passage as the rule of law when in fact it was taken from the dissenting opinion. The basic rule of thumb is, whereas creative construction of the law is permissible, construction of the law must not be fraudulent.

Many laypersons accuse legal professionals of using deceptive devices, loopholes in the law, and confusing legal terms in order to win. What these individuals fail to realize is that the advocate's job is to win. Clients have confidence in and pay that attorney whom they feel is best equipped to win. People who desire to lose certainly do not need to waste their time and money hiring an attorney. Rule 6 instructs all members of the legal profession that it is their ethical duty to win for their client, if at all legally possible. Legal professionals who do not use all of their faculties to do so betray a sacred and long-held trust.

FILE ONLY RIGHTEOUS CLAIMS WITH THE COURT

Whereas there is no definitive regulation that mandates that attorneys take every client who seeks their legal assistance (for instance, where the cause is so repugnant that they could not provide diligent legal assistance), once they have accepted the client, attorneys are compelled to argue any legal points on behalf of that client that have merit. The advocate role requires that the attorney argue for any claim that the attorney does not, after due consideration and investigation, consider to be without merit or frivolous.

Model Rule 3.1 says that a lawyer *shall not* bring or defend a *frivolous claim or contention.* This, of course, does not mean that only suits over existing law should be brought or defended against. Were that the case, new law would seldom be forged. What it does mean is that the lawyer must believe that the claim or cause has merit, even if it requires modification or reversal of existing law. Sometimes those are the best cases. The legal practitioner has a duty to use the legal system, not abuse it. This means both the substantive and procedural part of the law.

Abuse of process, the use of the process of the law for improper means, can be brought as a cross-complaint or countersuit in civil cases in many states. If the lawyer is named as a cross-complainant, it may mean that the lawyer must hire independent counsel for representation. In addition, a malicious prosecution suit can be brought after the conclusion of the frivolous suit. Therefore, it is the wise practitioner who considers all of the consequences of that lawsuit on the edge of frivolity.

In awarding sanctions against a lawyer for frivolous or bad faith tactics, the court should not look at one or two things, but the totality of the circumstances.[33] Where the plaintiff's law firm brought a claim that was worth $32 in the superior court by inflating the value with frivolous causes of action, and the suit was brought on a mechanics lien that had expired, the court had no problem finding that it was frivolous and brought for the sole purpose of harassment.[34] The penalties are severe.

*A **frivolous action** is one that is brought primarily for the purpose of harassment or where there is no good faith argument to support the action.*

GIFTS TO JUDGES

Model Rule 3.5 admonishes that the legal professional should not seek to influence a judge by any improper means. This includes gifts. Some judicial positions are now filled by way of election, however. How much of a campaign contribution can a legal professional make to a judge's campaign? Each professional might want to look this up in his or her state. Under some state's codes of judicial conduct, contributions to a campaign fund of a judge in any form are not permissible.

The giving of gifts or loans to members of the judiciary is prohibited to avoid the **appearance of impropriety** (Rule #10) as well as to avoid bias and prejudice. Commonsense exceptions may be where the judge is a family friend, in which case small exchanges of gifts during the holidays are not a violation of the Rule. Another exception may be where a judge has performed a marriage or other special ceremony, in which case a small token of appreciation is warranted.

If you're thinking about making a gift to a judge or other official, bear in mind that the purpose for the prohibition is to ensure impartiality. A gift or loan, therefore, must not be of such importance or size such that it would give rise to the argument that the integrity and impartiality of the judiciary are in question.

United States Supreme Court Justice Antonio Scalia came under fire in 2004 for going duck hunting with Vice President Dick Cheney shortly before the Supreme Court was to hear a case regarding Cheney's contact with certain Enron executives during the formulation of President Bush's energy policy. A lower court ruled that Cheney had to reveal certain documents. The Supreme Court agreed to hear Cheney's appeal. Surely their friendship would cause Justice Scalia to look at the case differently. Ethics scholar Stephan Gillers said of the hunting trip, "A judge may have a friendship with a lawyer, and that's fine. But if the lawyer has a case before the judge, they don't socialize until it's over. That shows a proper respect for maintaining the public's confidence in the integrity of the process."[35] The code of conduct for Federal Judges sets guidelines for members of the judiciary, but does not set clear-cut rules. "A judge should . . . act at all times in a manner that promotes public confidence in the integrity and impartiality of the judiciary," it says. "A judge should not allow family, social or other relationships to influence judicial conduct or judgments . . . or permit others to convey the impression that they are in a special position to influence the judge."

Despite what you may have seen in the news concerning Vice President Cheney vacationing with Supreme Court Justice Scalia, attorneys and their employees must not communicate with the Court during the pendency of a case unless a copy of the communication is promptly given to opposing counsel.[36] This rule applies to communications about the merits of the case and not to clerical issues.[37] Any attempt to solicit information on the merits of a case pending before that court from court personnel is prohibited.[38]

WHAT DO YOU THINK?

Your firm frequently practices law before Judge Scintilla. Scintilla's daughter is interviewing for a job as a paralegal with your firm. Would it be improper to hire her? Why or why not?

PROSECUTOR'S ROLE TO SEEK JUSTICE

We are supposed to be zealous in the representation of our clients. Unlike other attorneys, the prosecuting attorney's duty is not to win, but to reach a just result.[39] Prosecutors' clients are the public, the state, and the gov-

> Now might be a good time to pick up a copy of *My Cousin Vinny* and watch it. It's a comedic film about an inexperienced lawyer's first look at the criminal justice system. See how many unethical events or actions you can spot in the movie.

ernment, so they must be aware that public policy can be aided only by justice. They must utilize their best efforts to see that the guilty are convicted and the innocent do not suffer. While representing the public and the government, prosecutors must often make decisions that would be made by the client if the client were a private attorney. For that reason, prosecutors must always act in the best interests and with zealousness for the client: the public. They should construe all reasonable doubts in favor of the accused.

Prosecutors have the duty to make timely disclosure of any evidence or witnesses known to them that may tend to negate the defendant's guilt or mitigate punishment.[40]

The prosecution must disclose all substantial material evidence favorable to an accused.[41] For example, consider the case where the prosecutor did not disclose that the alleged victim was himself accused of filing false reports until after the preliminary hearings were held. Because the reports were "favorable to an accused" and pertinent to the credibility of a material witness, the prosecutor had a duty to provide the reports to the accused. The role of prosecuting attorneys is more than that of an *advocate*; their duty is not to obtain convictions, but to fully and fairly present to the court the evidence material to the charge on which the defendant stands trial.[42] This responsibility includes a duty to disclose to the defense substantial material evidence favorable to the accused in appropriate cases. This duty also encompasses the prosecuting attorney's duty to refrain from tactics that would be unethical if used by the accused's attorney.

advocate: One that argues for a cause.

RULE #6 WRAP-UP

The cornerstone of America's judicial system is "due process." We are guaranteed certain protections and procedures in the Constitution. Additionally, we are guaranteed the loyalty of the attorney we hire. As a paralegal, you owe each and every client that duty of loyalty and dedication and "zeal." But your zeal must stop before you break the law by such things as hiding or destroying evidence, fabricating evidence, and tampering with evidence, witnesses, or jurors. If you find out that your client will commit perjury or has committed perjury, you have certain obligations to the judicial system. This is true because the system has rights, too. You don't want to use deceit in your paralegal practice, and you don't want to let anyone else make you do something deceitful on behalf of a client. You want to be courteous and professional toward everyone, even when they don't remember that they are supposed to be courteous and professional to you. This courtesy and professionalism extend to the court, as well.

You cannot communicate directly with a represented person on the other side of litigation, and you cannot let that person communicate with you.

Remember that the prosecutor's role in the judicial system is different from the rest of the system. Despite what you may see on the nightly news, the prosecutor's job is to seek justice. If you go to work in the prosecutor's office, I promise you will always have an interesting job.

RULE #6 REVIEW QUESTIONS

1. What is "due process"? Why is it important in our judicial system?
2. What is "suppression of evidence"? Give some examples of how you might suppress evidence.
3. What is "fabricating evidence"? "Tampering with evidence"?
4. What is the difference between inducing a witness to testify falsely and allowing a witness to testify falsely? What is subornation of perjury?
5. If your client tells you that she intends to lie in her interrogatory responses, what should you do, step by step?
6. If your client tells you that she lied in her interrogatory responses, responses that were sent to opposing counsel long ago, what should you do, step by step?
7. If you are asked to lie about who you are in order to get information about one of your cases, what should you do?
8. Why is it important to be courteous to opposing counsel?
9. What is dicta and can you use it?
10. What is the prosecutor's job? How is it different from defense counsel's job?

---

1. *Powell v. Alabama,* 287 U.S. 45, 53 S.Ct. 55 (1932).
2. *Johns v. Smyth,* 176 F.Supp. 949 (E.D.Va. 1959).
3. Rule 6.2(a), EC 2-27.
4. Rule 6.2(a), EC 2-27.
5. Rule 6.2(a), EC 2-27.
6. In *People v. Belge,* 50 A.D.2d 1088, 376 N.Y.S.2d 771 (4th Dept. 1975), aff'd, 41 N.Y.2d 960, 390 N.Y.S.2d 867 (1976), a client informed his lawyer of the location of the corpses of young women the client had killed. The court held that the client's interest in confidentiality prevailed over the parents' interest in knowing their fate and the social interest in the proper treatment of the corpses.
7. *People v. Meredith,* 631 P.2d 46, 175 Cal. Rptr. 612 (Cal. 1981) (defense investigator removed victim's wallet from trash can as a result of client communication; held that prosecution entitled to be shown location of wallet, which was crucial to homicide prosecution); *State v. Olwell,* 394 P.2d 681, 64 Wash.2d 828 (1964) (counsel required to produce knife obtained from client over objection of attorney-client privilege).
8. See *People v. Meredith,* supra, and *State v. Olwell,* supra.
9. *Morrell v. State,* 575 P.2d 1200 (Alaska 1978) (kidnapping plan in defendant's handwriting properly turned over to authorities and lawyer required to answer source questions). *People v. Lee,* 3 Cal.App.3d 514, 83 Cal. Rptr. 715 (1970) (lawyer had no right to withhold shoes of client given by wife independently to lawyer).
10. See also *State v. Douglass,* 20 W.Va. 770 (1882), where the court held that lawyer's observations of the location of his client's pistol were protected by the attorney-client privilege. N.Y. Ethics Op. 479 (1978).

[11] *Sullins v. State Bar* 542 P.2d 631 (Cal. 1975).

[12] *Reznick v. State Bar,* 460 P.2d 969 (Cal. 1969).

[13] *State ex rel Nebraska State Bar v. Fisher,* 103 N.W.2d 325 (Neb. 1960).

[14] *In re Wright,* 248 P.2d 1080 (Nev. 1952).

[15] *Vaughn v. State Bar,* 2 Cal.Rptr. 11 (1960).

[16] *Smith v. State,* 523 S.W.2d 1 (Tex.App. 1975).

[17] *In re Howard,* 372 N.E.2d 371 (Ill. 1976).

[18] Rule 3.4(b) and EC 7-28.

[19] *Committee on Prof. Ethics and Conduct of the Iowa State Bar Assn. v. Crary,* 245 N.W.2d 298 (Iowa 1976), see also the lengthy Comments following Model Rule 3.3.

[20] *In re Bishop,* 210 S.E.2d 235 (S.C. 1974).

[21] *Iowa State Bar Assn. v. Hall,* 463 N.W.2d 30 (Iowa 1990).

[22] EC 7-30, Rule 4.4.

[23] EC 7-32.

[24] See Rule 3.4, Fairness to Opposing Counsel.

[25] See *Bates v. State Bar,* 275 Cal.Rptr. 381 (1990), and *Laguna Auto Body v. Farmers Ins. Exchange,* 282 Cal.Rptr. 530 (1991). In *Laguna Auto Body,* the court used the terminating sanction against counsel who abused the system.

[26] *Arrant v. State,* 537 So.2d 150 (Fla.App. 1989).

[27] *In re Elam,* 211 S.W.2d 710, *cert. denied,* 335 U.S. 872, 69 S.Ct. 161 (1948).

[28] *Leimer v. Hulse,* 178 S.W.2d 336, *rein. denied,* 323 U.S. 744, 65 S.Ct. 60 (1944).

[29] *State v. Turner,* 538 P.2d 966 (Kan. 1975).

[30] *Runsvold v. Idaho State Bar,* 925 F.2d 1118 (Idaho 1996); Rule 4.2.

[31] *Hill v. Houpt,* 141 A. 159 (Pa. 1929).

[32] *Fouls v. Maryland Casualty Co.,* 30 F.2d 357 (1929).

[33] *West Coast Devel. v. Read,* 3 Cal.Rptr.2d 709 (1992).

[34] *Id.*

[35] *Los Angeles Times* (January 17, 2004).

[36] *Heavey v. State Bar,* 551 P.2d 1238 (Cal. 1976).

[37] *Stern Bros., Inc. v. McClure,* 236 S.E.2d 222 (W.Va. 1977).

[38] *Matter of J.B.K.,* 931 S.W.2d 581 (Tex.App. 1996).

[39] Model Rule 3.8; *People v. Zimmer,* 414 N.E.2d 705 (N.Y. 1980).

[40] EC 7-13; *People v. Ruthford,* 534 P.2d 1341 (Cal. 1975).

[41] *Currie v. Superior Court,* 281 Cal.Rptr. 250 (1991).

[42] Rule 3.8.

DON'T PRACTICE LAW WITHOUT A LICENSE

WHAT IS THE UNAUTHORIZED PRACTICE OF LAW?

The unauthorized practice of law (UPL) and its relationship to access to justice are two of the most complex challenges in legal ethics today. Although it is every legal professional's duty to protect the public from unskilled or unscrupulous practitioners, the practice of law has traditionally been restricted to only licensed attorneys. Attorneys must have a certain amount of education and pass a bar exam. Attorneys are regulated by their state bar associations or court system so the public has some assurance that it will be protected from unqualified, negligent, or dishonest attorneys. However, the vast majority of the public will not be able to afford to hire a lawyer when the need arises. So, when we discuss UPL, we discuss that delicate balance of **protecting the public** and **access to justice (Rule #5).** The conflict created by these two concerns makes choices about UPL more difficult than ever before. Therefore, when trying to determine what is the unauthorized practice of law, we look at both what will best protect the public from unqualified people making important legal decisions and what will leave room for legal assistance for those presently without representation.

Why Should Only Lawyers Practice Law?

The Model Rules of Professional Conduct state the following:

> Rule 5.5: A lawyer shall not: (a) practice in a jurisdiction where doing so violates the regulation of the legal profession in that jurisdiction; or (b) assist a person who is not a member of the bar in the performance of activity that constitutes the unauthorized practice of law.

> ABA Mode Code EC 3-1: The prohibition against the practice of law by a layman is grounded in the need of the public for integrity and competence of those who render legal services. Because of the fiduciary and personal character of the lawyer-client relationship and the inherently complex nature of our legal system, the public can better be assured of the requisite responsibility and competence if the practice of law is confined to those who are subject to the requirements and regulations imposed upon members of the legal profession.

Note that this Rule is two-fold: it is improper to practice law without a license, and it is improper to assist another in doing so. For all the discussion, however, the ABA, the state bar associations, and the courts have been reluctant to set a definite standard for what, exactly, constitutes the practice of law. (The ABA actually said in its earlier Model Code that it was "neither necessary nor desirable to attempt the formulation of a single, specific definition of what constitutes the practice of law. It is a matter for determination by the courts of that jurisdiction."[1]) Leaving it to the courts to decide, then, means that what activities constitute the practice of law will be determined jurisdiction by jurisdiction, activity by activity. As a result, the law on the unauthorized practice of law is changing continually and is different in every jurisdiction. As a paralegal, you are responsible for complying with legal authority governing the unauthorized practice of law in your own jurisdiction.

Why Should We Care?

The unauthorized practice of law is one of the greatest concerns to those entering the paralegal field. It is also of concern to lawyers and people who are currently in law school or are awaiting positive bar exam results. It is very easy to "practice law" inadvertently, even innocently. The public interest is at stake, though, as well the legal profession and its reputation, so the courts and bar associations are not forgiving of violators.

We Really Do Know What the Practice of Law Is

Activities to be aware of in the unauthorized practice of law fall into four categories: (1) prohibitions on the practice of law by nonlawyers, (2) lawyers aiding the unauthorized practice of law, (3) the responsibility of lawyers for their nonlawyer personnel, and (4) misrepresentations by nonlawyers as to their status. The ABA Model Codes and Model Rules, state and federal laws, a tradition of case-by-case determination, and the various state bar associations' opinions all contribute to the diverse points of view in all four areas. In this chapter, we will address all of these categories in order. Our objective is to define the "practice of law" with sufficient particularity so that the student will be able to avoid all activities that are "unauthorized." The goal is to protect the public while providing access to justice for everyone.

PROHIBITIONS ON THE PRACTICE OF LAW BY NONATTORNEYS

The general rule is that the practice of law is limited to those who are licensed and admitted to the bar after satisfying certain state requirements with regard to education, moral character, and examination: a licensed attorney or lawyer. Not the least of all of the considerations concerning those who are licensed to practice law is that these people are subject to the profession's disciplinary regulations. Those people who have not been qualified as attorneys but who, nevertheless, seek to practice law may be subject to civil penalties or, in some states, criminal penalties.

The activities that constitute the "unauthorized practice of law" are subject to the interpretation of each state. That means that there is no universal standard. Most states provide no definition but other states have laid the foundation for some common themes on a case-by-case basis. Some of the more common expressions you will see are the following:

1. Is the activity one "traditionally practiced by lawyers"?[2]
2. Is it "commonly understood" to involve the practice of law?[3]
3. Does it "require legal skill or knowledge beyond that of a layperson"?[4]
4. Is it "characterized by the personal relationship between attorney and client"?[5]
5. Is this activity one that "the public interest is best served by limiting performance to those who are attorneys"?[6]

The problem with all of these definitions is that they are rather vague and are based on tradition. In our quickly changing society, maybe "tradition" isn't the best standard.

All states have statutes that limit the practice of law to licensed attorneys. By now, you should know where to locate these statutes in your state law. In most states, these statutes say only something not helpful such as "those without a license cannot practice law," and the courts are left the

You should familiarize yourself with your state's law for enforcing the unauthorized practice of law regulations. A good place to start your research may be West's Digest Topic "Attorney & Client," key number 11(13).

A Google search of the term "unauthorized practice of law" will turn up thousands of resources!

task of interpreting those words. The few states that attempt to define the acts that constitute the *practice of law* generally refer to three broad categories of activity:

1. Representing others before judicial or administrative bodies[7]
2. Preparing legal documents which affect the legal rights of others[8]
3. Advising others with regard to their legal rights[9]

1. Representing Others as UPL

In *State ex rel. Stephan v. Williams,*[10] the nonlawyer signed pleadings, made appearances and examined witnesses. That's got to be clearly UPL. Appearing in court to represent another person is one of the obvious signs of UPL.

Even though we might think otherwise, because a husband cannot be *in pro per* for himself and his wife, representing his wife is UPL.[11]

Even attempting to help a client in requesting a continuance in some of the more conservative states is UPL.[12] This may seem like overkill because asking for a continuance doesn't have any substantive law implications, but it is an appearance in court on behalf of another person—and only a licensed attorney may do that.

In pro per is short for in propria persona. That is Latin for representing yourself.

2. Preparing Legal Documents as UPL

There have been a number of cases on secretarial services preparing legal documents as the unauthorized practice of law. Even the early ones held that selling legal documents and preparing them for a fee are not improper so long as the information typed has been written out first by the client, or it is typed at the instruction of the client.[13] However, in *Florida Bar v. Furman,* the Florida court seemingly overturned that decision late in 1984 by convicting Rosemary Furman, the owner-operator of a secretarial service specializing in legal forms, of practicing law without a license based on its opinion that her "relationship" with her client was like that of attorney-client. She was sentenced to 120 days in jail, ninety of which would be waived if she would not violate the court's order and refrain from typing legal forms. The case began in 1979.[14]

Drafting the simplest complaint and uncomplicated petition for dissolution (divorce) without the oversight of an attorney is UPL.[15] In other words, drafting legal documents (number 2 above) is the practice of law unless the drafter is supervised by an attorney.

Obviously, if the paralegal is preparing legal documents at the request of a lawyer, this is not UPL. Preparing legal documents is what paralegals are supposed to do! The courts have created a legal fiction to explain this. They say that where the supervising attorney approves of the work product (such as by signing it) that "he adopts [it] as his own."[16]

In *In re Calzadilla,* 151 B.R. 622 (Fla. 1993), the bankruptcy court ruled that secretarial services may sell printed materials and sample forms and type bankruptcy forms from written information provided by clients and they may advertise these services. They may not, however, advise how best to fill out the forms or assist in filling out schedules. They may not "correct" what they believe to be errors by the patron. They also may not use the word "paralegal" in their advertising material as that may mislead reasonable laypeople into believing that they are permitted to provide legal assistance.

3. Advising Others and Books and Kits as UPL

If you sat down with your friend, listened to her story of the awful thing that has happened to her, and proceeded to explain her legal rights to her, you would be "practicing law" because you are using your legal knowledge and skill, applying it to her specific facts and giving her advice. That part seems clear. Paralegals, even though they may be very knowledgeable about the law, cannot share that knowledge by helping others with their legal problems—not even your best friend; not even for free; not even if you begin with the disclaimer "I'm not allowed to practice law, but . . . "; and not even if you write it down and give it to her or point out the answer to her in a book. Those are the three elements to look for: using your knowledge of the law, applying it to a particular person's fact pattern, and giving a conclusion or opinion.

Although it doesn't seem like writing a book could be UPL because books do not address individuals' fact patterns, some states have put this to the test.[17] Most courts have applied a "personal relationship between attorney and client" test to books like *How to Avoid Probate* and the *Divorce Yourself Kit.* Surely people need these books and use them successfully every day. Holding that they violate state UPL statutes would mean taking them off the public library shelves and out of the bookstores. The need for access to justice would not be met that way. No litigation to ban these books has been successful.

The consensus of the courts is that such kits are not the unauthorized practice of law so long as they are sold to the general public and the seller does not answer questions relating to specific individuals. Companies selling a kit <u>and</u> personal legal services have been shut down by the various law enforcement agencies. For example, in late 1997, a "trust mill" in California was closed after a state bar investigation revealed that nonlawyers were selling living trust "packages" on behalf of a lawyer. The sales agents used a sample living trust that they promised to customize for each purchaser.[18] So, actually meeting with the client creates that "personal relationship" and crosses the line between UPL and access to justice.

Look for *U.S. v. Johnson* on the publisher's Web site. What do you think about the services Mr. Robinson and NLPA provided to Mr. Johnson? Shouldn't the defendant have the right to decide what legal services will serve him best?

> In *Statewide Grievance Committee v. Patton* 683 A.2d 1359 (Conn. 1996), the court shut down an organization called Doc-U-Prep. The defendant in that case gave customers a form to fill out and sent the form to the Doc-U-Prep headquarters in Massachusetts. That organization completed the forms with the information provided and returned the completed documents to the defendant who delivered them to the customers. All of the legal forms were for uncontested matters such as a will, corporation, or name change, but included Chapter 7 bankruptcy, a subject in which many legal technicians practice as Bankruptcy Petition Preparers (BPPs). The court overruled all of the defendants. First Amendment freedom of speech, Fourteenth Amendment equal protection and due process challenges, holding that "prohibiting unsupervised paralegals from work with legal consequences is rationally related to public protection."

However, kits and books that the consumer can purchase and receive no in-person legal advice are not UPL. Even as recently as 1999 this was tested in Texas where the state bar tried to ban the sale of Nolo Press books as UPL.

WHAT IS NOT UPL

Overlapping Functions—Not UPL

Some activities, while they look like the practice of law by laypeople, are authorized by the law. These activities can be performed by both lawyers and nonlawyers so they are often referred to as "overlapping functions." Some of the most obvious rights and activities involving overlapping functions are:

1. The right to lay participation in the exercise of certain federally protected rights[19]
2. The right of nonattorneys to representation before federal administrative agencies[20]
3. The right of indigent criminal defendants to representation by law students[21]
4. The right of nonattorneys to self-representation[22]
5. Lay practice before state administrative agencies[23]

"Incidental to"—Not UPL

Some statutes specifically permit certain groups of individuals and certain organizations to practice law because it's just a little bit of law and unavoidable. We call these the "incidental to" businesses:

1. Preparation of instruments by title companies and real estate brokers[24]
2. Estate planning by banks and insurance agencies[25]
3. Debt collection by commercial agencies[26]
4. Tax practice by accountancy agencies[27]

You can see the obvious problem that these "incidental to" businesses face. They are allowed to give some limited legal advice because it is incidental to their ordinary course of business. They must be careful not to cross the line into the blatant practice of law. As no one can tell them exactly where that line is, it's difficult to know what is lawful and what is not. Most of these industries stick to the bits of "practicing law" that they have been doing for many years (the "tradition" standard again) so they avoid trouble. Periodically, however, when they branch out, they are accused of UPL violations.

Doing Your Job—Not UPL

Paralegals who are doing their job "prepare legal documents," but it is not UPL because it is done under the supervision of a lawyer. Paralegals perform legal research and share the answers with clients, but this is not UPL because it is done at the behest of a lawyer. South Carolina, in a case heard by its supreme court, set the following standard for permissible paralegal activities:

> Paralegals are routinely employed by licensed attorneys to assist in the preparation of legal documents such as deeds and mortgages. The activities of a paralegal do not constitute the practice of law *as long as they are limited to work of a preparatory nature, such as legal research, investigation, or the composition of legal documents,* which enable the licensed attorney-employer to carry a given matter to a conclusion through his own examination, approval, or additional effort.[28] (Emphasis added.)

What about Disbarred or Suspended Lawyers?

In *Florida Bar v. Thomson*[29] the Florida Supreme Court held that attorneys suspended from the practice of law may perform law clerk (paralegal) work in an office during their suspension. In describing the duties such a person could perform, the court said:

> [He] limited his functions exclusively to work of a preparatory nature such as research, taking statements of witnesses consistent with initial investigation of a case, assembling information for review, and like work that would enable the attorney-employer to carry a given matter to a conclusion through his own examination, approval, or additional effort. *He adds that all of his activities have been*

> *performed under the direct supervision of the attorney-employer, and that he has not held himself out to be an attorney, has not signed any pleadings or letter in behalf of any attorney, has made no court appearances, has had no direct contact with any client or given any legal advice to any client, and has conducted himself in the sole role of research investigator for his employer.* (Emphasis added.)

> We also find the services allegedly performed by Thomson in his capacity as a law clerk or investigator similar to those performed by paraprofessionals or paralegals in this state and elsewhere.

There have been opinions to the contrary based on the theory that such a disbarred or suspended attorney would not be able to refrain from practicing law. Other opinions state that disbarred or suspended attorneys should be separated from the practice of law entirely for the protection of the public.

Prohibitions under Scrutiny

Prohibitions on the practice of law by nonattorneys are subject to criticism on policy grounds by attorneys and lay people. These prohibitions have been challenged on First Amendment, due process, and antitrust theories. They have been called paternalistic and self-serving.[30] Studies show that very few of the UPL prosecutions and civil cases involve actual injury to a member of the public and that, in many instances, lawyer intervention is much more costly for the public and the service provided is substantially slower. In other words, there is a vast segment of society that needs legal assistance but cannot afford a lawyer. When a member of the public gets good assistance from a nonlawyer who is practicing law in violation of the UPL laws, nothing happens. However, when a member of the public is harmed and makes a complaint to the district attorney or the bar, an investigation may or may not be initiated, and the nonlawyer may or may not continue in business, harming other people.

Primary in the Model Rules and Model Code of the ABA are two suppositions: (1) that the public is best served by maintaining the high standards of quality achieved by self-regulation and (2) that only licensed attorneys should be subject to regulation by the ethical considerations. In other words, the organized bar believes that both the effective administration of the legal system and the interests of the clients as consumers of legal services can be provided for in a single set of standards governing attorney conduct. To achieve this, there are statutes, cases, and bar regulations to be considered.

What Is the Effect of UPL?

The public is often harmed by UPL. *In re McCarthy*[31] is a good illustration of the consequences of the potential harm UPL causes to the public in a bankruptcy setting. In that case, the debtor was not well-served by nonattorney representation resulting in a great financial loss to her. In addition, because she was not represented by a lawyer, she had no way to get her money back through a legal malpractice case. Obviously, lawyers and nonlawyers can make mistakes that ultimately harm the client. However, lawyers can be sued for malpractice; nonlawyers cannot. Where there is a pattern of below-standard legal work, lawyers may be subject to discipline. Again, nonlawyers are exempt from state bar regulations.

Exceptions to General UPL Rules

There are, of course, exceptions to the prohibition on the practice of law by nonlawyers and, because determinations in this area have been made on an ad hoc, case-by-case basis, the exceptions vary greatly among the jurisdictions. There are, however, common themes and exceptions established as a matter of constitutional right that are universally recognized by the states. These exceptions permit self-representation, lay participation in certain administrative proceedings, lay participation in the exercise of federally protected rights, and law student practice, especially in the area of indigent representation.

Self-representation. The right of self-representation in federal courts is codified in 28 USC § 1654:

> In all courts of the United States the parties may plead and conduct their own cases personally or by counsel as, by the rules of such courts, respectively, are permitted to manage and conduct causes therein.

Law students. In *People v. Perez,*[32] the California Supreme Court held that valuable practical training and increasing the availability of legal services for indigent people were strong enough reasons to permit "limited practice of law" by law students, providing they are properly supervised. Of course, the states vary immensely as to in what area and under what circumstances law students may practice law. All states that allow law students to represent others, however, include adequate supervision caveats, permit appearances at special administrative hearings and preparation of legal documents, set specifications as to the educational background of the student, and provide for the student's proper introduction to the court.[33]

Faretta v. California, 422 U.S. 806, 75 S.Ct. 2625 (1975) brought the right of self-representation to the states when it was upheld by the Supreme Court as a constitutional right in criminal cases. Ethical Consideration 3-7 of the ABA Model Code reads: ". . . anyone who does not wish to avail himself of [educated legal] representation is not required to do so."

Using the "access to the courts" theory, the federal government has allowed paralegals and law students to represent others in Medicaid, food stamp, and unemployment compensation matters. Likewise, indigent prisoners have been utilizing nonattorneys since 1969 under the same theory.[34] In the strides made for the use of paralegals in representing indigents, prisoners, and others who may not have adequate representation, the concurring opinion of Justice Douglas has been cited again and again:

> The increasing complexities of our governmental apparatus at both the local and the federal levels have made it difficult for a person to process a claim or even to make a complaint. . . . [I]t is becoming abundantly clear that more and more of the effort in ferreting out the basis of claims and the agencies responsible for them and in preparing the almost endless paperwork for their prosecution is work for laymen. There are not enough lawyers to manage or supervise all of these affairs; and much of the basic work done requires no special legal talent. Yet there is a closed-shop philosophy in the legal profession that cuts down drastically active roles for laymen. That traditional, closed-shop attitude is utterly out of place in the modern world where claims pile high and much of the work of tracing and pursuing them requires the patience and wisdom of a layman rather than the legal skills of a member of the bar. . . . (at 491)

Administrative agencies. Many federal agencies permit lay representation.[35] The National Labor Relations Board and other administrative bodies allow any layperson to represent others before them, whereas other agencies, such as the Patent Office and the ICC, require specific educational qualifications and the passing of an examination. With regard to state administrative agencies, however, there is a great deal of inconsistency. Some state courts have even ruled that the state legislature has no power to authorize practice before agencies created by the legislature. Others have followed the Florida ruling in *Florida Bar v. Moses*,[36] which held that the legislature and the judiciary have concurrent authority in this area and either may make such rules to assist the public in attaining adequate representation.

The United States Supreme Court has held that the states have no authority to regulate lay representation before federal agencies under the supremacy clause of the Constitution.[37] Likewise, the United States Supreme Court has held that the states could not interfere if the lay representation was the only alternative to protect federally guaranteed rights. As previously discussed, the Supreme Court held that in the preparation of various petitions for postconviction relief, inmates were allowed to furnish assistance to other inmates who were poorly educated and unable to retain counsel.

Some examples, just to name a few, of federal law allowing nonlawyer representation are the following:

> Small Business Administration [13 CFR 121.11, 134.16]
> National Credit Union Administration [12 CFR 747]
> Federal Energy Regulatory Commission [18 CFR 385.2101]
> Drug Enforcement Administration [21 CFR 1316.50]
> Aid to Families with Dependent Children [45 CFR 205]
> Food and Drug Administration [32 CFR 12.40, 12.45]
> Comptroller of the Currency [12 CFR 19.3]
> Immigration and Naturalization Service [8 CFR 292.1-3]
> Environmental Protection Agency [40 CFR 124, 164.30, 22.10]

What Is Definitely Not "Giving Legal Advice"

Working in the field of law requires common sense. A commonsense approach to UPL will prevent you from becoming paralyzed by the fear of violating one of what seems to be an infinite list of rules. In the traditional law office setting, you will often hear a lawyer say to a paralegal, "Call Client X and tell her. . . " Even if the paralegal is instructed to give Client X what would technically be called "legal advice," that the advice is given by the paralegal does not mean that it is UPL. The paralegal is simply acting as a *conduit of the legal advice* from the lawyer to the client, just as if the lawyer had written the advice in a letter and sent it to the client. The conduit theory, then, covers most instances of the paralegal giving legal advice to the client.

Ordinarily, the paralegal has been instructed in what to say—that's why we can call it the conduit theory. Sometimes, however, the paralegal has been told what to say to one client in one circumstance and would now like to give that same advice to a different client in a similar circumstance. Here the line begins to blur. In certain circumstances, it may be permissible to give the advice to the client and in others it may not. In yet other circumstances, it may be acceptable to say, "This is what I think the answer is, but I'm going to check with a lawyer and if the answer isn't right, I'll call you back." In that way, the client has gotten a more immediate answer, the paralegal has been helpful, and the paralegal is going to discuss the question with that conduit-lawyer to verify the answer.[38]

Corporations

Corporations present a special problem because they are not "persons" as we traditionally think of them. Therefore, corporations cannot utilize the right of self-representation. Most states agree that a corporation must be represented by a lawyer in a court of law but nonlawyers can represent them in administrative proceedings.[39] So it is UPL for the nonlawyer president of a corporation to file and answer in a court and prosecute an appeal.[40]

> **WHAT DO YOU THINK?**
>
> In a Florida Bar Advisory Opinion, 627 So.2d 485 (1993), Florida, traditionally very hard on UPL offenders, opined that a nonlawyer property manager could represent the individual or corporate landlord in uncontested residential evictions, so long as the authority was given to the property manager in writing and the action did not involve a judgment for past rent. Isn't the property manager practicing law without a license? Why should (or shouldn't) an exception be made for this instance?

Paralegals working in corporations face interesting UPL problems when they are not working under the supervision of lawyers. With recent corporate cutbacks, it is now commonplace to see a corporate legal department staffed solely with paralegals. When the corporate paralegal is asked for legal advice by someone in the corporation, does she or he commit UPL by responding? The answer is maybe, depending upon the nature of the question. An employee of a corporation doesn't really have a "client" in the typical sense of the word—just other employees. If we liken this paralegal's position to that of the typical personnel manager, who is often called upon to answer legal questions regarding personnel issues, then it is not UPL; the answer to the legal question is incidental to the person's primary job. If the corporate paralegal's primary job is coordinating outside legal counsel, when the paralegal is asked "What do you advise we do in the Brown case?" by a corporate officer, the paralegal's response "Take Mr. Brown's deposition" is not necessarily UPL. Who's the client?

LAWYERS AIDING THE UNAUTHORIZED PRACTICE OF LAW

Attorneys can violate the regulations that prohibit their aiding the unauthorized practice of law by improperly supervising their employees and associates, by allowing a nonlawyer to influence their independent professional judgment (dividing fees), or by entering into an improper business relationship with a nonlawyer. We discuss each one in order.

Improper Supervision

Earlier we talked about paralegals preparing legal documents that are then accepted by the lawyer, and so the task of preparing legal documents is not UPL. The theory is that the lawyer will read the document and "adopt it as his own." But what happens when the lawyer is not reading the documents? What if your supervising lawyer signs the documents

For an almost amusing case, read *In re Schelly,* 446 N.E.2d 236 (Ill. 1983), in which a lawyer employed a disbarred attorney as a law clerk and even after having been repeatedly disciplined by the bar and the court for allowing this clerk to practice law, the attorney continued to employ the clerk, and the clerk continued to try cases when his supervising attorney instructed him to ask the court for continuances. Finally, the court charged the attorney with aiding his employee in the unauthorized practice of law and failure to supervise and convicted him of not restricting or supervising his law clerk.

without reading them? By failing to properly supervise nonlawyer staff members, lawyers break the law by aiding in the unauthorized practice of law. The point of having the lawyer do legal work is to ensure that the public gets educated, trained, responsible, and regulated lawyers performing this important work. When the lawyer doesn't do the lawyer's job, and leaves the job to a paralegal who is unsupervised, the public is not getting the protection that the law has designed.

This is also true in the case of contract or independent or freelance paralegals doing work in an area in which the lawyer has no expertise. For example, the real estate lawyer hires a probate paralegal to handle the probates that come into the office. The lawyer hires the paralegal not because there is too much work or he simply doesn't want to perform the probate work, but because he doesn't know how to do probate work. If this is the case, the real estate lawyer cannot supervise that paralegal because she or he has no knowledge of probate law. This improper (or absent) supervision constitutes UPL.

Improper Division of Fees

The law says, quite simply, that lawyers must not divide fees with nonlawyers. This is because the law has long believed that no one but lawyers should make decisions about legal matters. If nonlawyers are eligible to profit financially from legal matters, their influence will poison the relationship of trust between lawyer and client. So, for this reason, paralegals who refer clients to their employing law firms cannot get "a piece of the action." Furthermore, paralegals cannot have an employment contract that states that the salary will be based on the outcome of the case or the profits of the firm.[41] To pay such a fee would be a violation of UPL standards. This law, however, does not mandate that employees be paid a fixed salary. Bonuses, annual or more frequent, are perfectly permitted, so long as the bonus is not based on a percentage of the law firm profits or a percentage of a particular legal fee.

In *Atkins v. Tinning*, 865 S.W.2d 533 (Tex. 1993), the court found that such an agreement is illegal for the lawyer only, as the prohibitions on fee splitting apply only to lawyers. The court awarded the nonlawyer his share under the agreement and disciplined the lawyer. Note that illegal referral fees are ordinarily held to be illegal for both parties and will therefore not be enforced by the court.[42]

Improper Business Relationship

ABA Model Rule 5.4(b) prohibits lawyers and nonlawyers from being in business together if any part of that business will be the practice of law. Historically, this was to prevent a nonlawyer from having any say about the outcome of a legal matter. An exception is made to this rule for group legal service providers such as NAACP and the ACLU. Another exception is labor unions.

In the everyday practice of law, however, this rule is still in place. For example, consider the case in which a lawyer introduced a person to his clients and told them that this person was an attorney who was licensed in another state and had practiced law in Europe. Thereafter, this person consulted with the clients without the supervision of the lawyer. Notwithstanding the contention that the unlicensed person was only assisting the clients in obtaining counsel in Europe and that he actually rendered no legal assistance, the lawyer was held to have aided the nonlawyer in the unauthorized practice of law. Further, the court held that since the two individuals shared fees on a regular basis, theirs was an improper business relationship.[43]

This Rule, and the Rules on lawyers and nonlawyers not sharing fees, are subject to criticism by those organizations that are trying to make access to the judicial system more affordable. To that end, in 1990, the District of Columbia modified the ABA version of Rule 5.4 to allow partnerships between lawyers and nonlawyers.[44] This arrangement allows the lawyer and paralegal to pool their resources to start a law firm. It also allows the paralegal to work with, not for, the lawyer. This relationship will benefit the public by making the judicial system more attainable.

THE LAWYER'S RESPONSIBILITY FOR NONLAWYER PERSONNEL

Lawyers are responsible for the conduct of their employees. This is *respondeat superior,* or let the master answer. This rule dates back to 1747 when the Court of Chancery held that the solicitor must answer to his client for the negligence of his clerk as if it were his own act.[45] Similarly, in 1902 an American court held that attorneys would be liable for the intentional criminal acts of their clerks against the attorneys and their clients.[46]

Supervision and Hiring

Because the lawyer is responsible for the acts of his or her paralegal, Rule 5.3 of the ABA Rules of Professional Conduct unquestionably makes the employer-attorney responsible for the unethical conduct of the paralegal. That the employer must make reasonable efforts to see that paralegal's conduct conforms with the ethical obligations of the lawyer is also clearly stated in this Rule. Exactly what are "reasonable efforts" and what is conforming conduct for the paralegal is a moving target. A simple rule of thumb, however, is this: paralegals may not do anything that would be unethical if done by a lawyer. Attorneys cannot accomplish an unethical end by having their employees perform the actual unethical act.

Lawyers who employ paralegals must ensure, for example, that the paralegals know their obligations under the duty of confidentiality. You already know your duty, but other paralegals may not, so the law puts the burden on the attorney to provide training in the rules of professional responsibility.

The court will sanction the supervising attorney who uses the paralegal improperly, such as the case where the attorney authorized his nonattorney employee to sign the attorney's name to a bankruptcy petition. The court found that there had been no participation by the attorney in the bankruptcy filing. The court sanctioned the attorney the moving party's attorney's fees. Typically the court will cite ABA Opinion 316 (1967) authorizing the use of nonlawyer assistants "so long as it is [the lawyer] who takes the work and vouches for it to the client and becomes responsible to the client."

In *Matter of Martinez*,[47] the court found that the paralegal's failure to identify himself as a nonlawyer, quoting legal fees, and cashing a settlement

In *Louisiana State Bar Assn. v. Edwins*, 540 So.2d 294 (La. 1989), a disciplinary proceeding, the court found that a paralegal independently operated a branch office for Attorney Edwins. The paralegal (Robertson) told clients he was an attorney, quoted legal fees, prepared pleadings and signed Attorney Edwins's name, and had exclusive control over an account where client settlement checks were deposited. Robertson completed the client's matter without the client ever meeting the attorney. In determining if Edwins knew about Robertson's activities, the court considered Robertson's letterhead: "Now you can have a lawyer too ... through Prepaid Legal Services, Rob Robertson" (at 301). Moreover, the client Robertson "helped" had no input as to the settlement and no meaningful explanation of the distribution of the settlement funds. Attorney Edwins was disbarred when the court found that he had improperly "delegated the exercise of his professional judgment" to the legal assistant.

check payable to the client with no supporting documentation constituted improper conduct. The attorney's failure to identify his assistant as a non-lawyer was the attorney's improper conduct, and all of the improper conduct of the paralegal was *imputed* to the attorney by virtue of the lawyer's duty to supervise his employee to ensure that the conduct of his assistant comported with the attorney's own professional obligations.

*To **impute** means to attribute fault or responsibility to someone else.*

Delegation

A lawyer may delegate work that does not require the exercise of professional judgment to paralegals. Tasks that require giving legal advice (other than conveying information received from the attorney), representing clients in courts, or signing legal documents may not be delegated because these tasks are reserved to attorneys as "the practice of law."[48]

What this means from a practical standpoint is that it is often the paralegal's responsibility to say "no" to a lawyer who tries to delegate an improper task. For example, although it may be acceptable for a lawyer to instruct the paralegal to sign the lawyer's name to an enclosure letter, it is not acceptable to ask the paralegal to sign the lawyer's name to a pleading. As another example, it is an accepted practice to send a paralegal to a deposition to take notes and observe in place of a lawyer, but it would be UPL for the paralegal to ask questions of the deponent or otherwise actively participate in the deposition. Proper delegation enables the legal profession to bring legal services to the public more economically and efficiently. Improper delegation can be UPL.

MISREPRESENTATION

Those states that have taken steps to regulate the activities of paralegals have taken greatest interest in ensuring that paralegals will not be mistaken for attorneys. In order to protect the public from innocent mistakes regarding the identity of paralegals and those tasks they may perform, several states have made regulations pertaining to the image projected by paralegals. For example, states disagree on whether paralegals can be listed on letterhead stationery and telephone directories. The supervising lawyer will ultimately be responsible for errors. Some states allow paralegal names listed on letterhead stationery so long as it clearly says "paralegal" under the name. The point is to make sure that members of the public do not mistake a paralegal for a lawyer.

As a paralegal, you will probably be given your own business card. Under your name, it should say "paralegal" or "legal assistant" or whatever your designation might be. It cannot say nothing at all because anyone looking at a law firm business card will assume that the person listed there is a lawyer. Lawyers do not have to put the word "lawyer" on their business cards (although they usually do), but paralegals must have their nonlawyer status designated in some way.

WHAT DO YOU THINK?

If your business card must say "paralegal" on it, what about the sign on your office door? Will members of the public who see your office door think that you are a lawyer?

ENFORCEMENT OF UPL REGULATIONS

Injunction, criminal prosecution, citation for contempt of court, and writs of quo warranto are the most widely used methods of enforcement of the unauthorized practice regulations. Nearly all jurisdictions have misdemeanor statutes, although it is maintained that injunctive relief is the most effective method for stopping the offender.

With regard to who may initiate the proceeding for an injunction, many states allow suits by the *integrated bar*. Those that allow class actions by attorneys require a showing of irreparable injury or some proof that the attorneys represent the public interest. Suits that have attempted to prevent the unauthorized practice of law on the theory that attorneys have the exclusive right to practice law and, therefore, the right to be protected from competition from unlicensed people, are steeped in antitrust problems. This theory, furthermore, does not consider that the prohibition on the unauthorized practice of law is to protect the public from incompetent representation, not to protect attorneys from competition.

Criminal contempt citations have been called an overreaction to a trivial problem but they are, nevertheless, common. The direct citation, one closely connected to the court or a pending case, can be issued by the court on its own motion. For those activities that occur without the court's knowledge, an indirect citation may be sought by the state attorney general, a bar association, or an individual attorney upon a petition to the court.

Quo warranto writs are used to restrain corporations from exceeding their chartered purposes. This action is brought by the attorney general on behalf of the public to prevent corporations from practicing law incident to their primary purpose or business. An example of this is where the attorney general seeks to prevent real estate brokers from giving legal advice or filling out certain real estate documents for their customers as part of their ordinary business.

*Have we defined **integrated bar** yet? I don't think so. An integrated bar is a bar association that has mandatory membership of all lawyers. For example, California has an integrated bar meaning that you can't practice law in California unless you are a member of the California Bar.*

***Quo warranto** is Latin for by what authority. The writ asks "by what authority are you practicing law" and asks for the "cease and desist" remedy.*

An Illinois appellate court held that there is no private cause of action for a violation of Illinois' unauthorized practice statute unless the allegations were of negligence or the defendants had actually held themselves out to be attorneys (*Torres v. Fiol*, 441 N.E.2d 1300 [Ill.App. 1982]).

> Effective October 1, 2004, practicing law without a license in Florida (including "holding out" oneself as a lawyer) is a third degree felony punishable by up to five years imprisonment and a fine of up to $5,000, Fla.Stat. sec. 454.23. Similarly, a disbarred or suspended lawyer who practices law is guilty of a felony, Fla.Stat. 454.31. The Florida Bar supported the new laws, but did not initiate them.

There are other ways to prevent or stop the unauthorized practice of law found in tort[49] and in contract,[50] but the truth is that very little is done to prevent "true" unauthorized practice of law (the practice of law by people who have never been trained in law) because, at least in some part, the offense is a crime and the criminal justice system is overwhelmed with crimes considered more important.

RULE #7 WRAP-UP

So, now we completely understand what the practice of law is, when it's not okay to do it, how we might do it inadvertently, and what the penalties are, right? We now know that the practice of law comes in three colors: representing others, preparing legal documents, and giving legal advice. We looked at a plain and simple, easy-to-apply rule for what is giving legal advice: using your knowledge of the law, applying it to a particular person's facts, and drawing a conclusion or opinion. Letting attorneys not properly supervise you is a good way to violate the "preparing legal documents" rule of UPL. Even though paralegals can "prepare" legal documents, an attorney must review and approve them. And, we now know that there are lots of agencies that allow lay practice so, if you're not interested in the "traditional" paralegal path of working for lawyers, there are other places where your legal skill and knowledge can be put to good use—helping the public.

RULE #7 REVIEW QUESTIONS

1. What are the two competing concerns for the public that make unauthorized practice of law choices so difficult? How would you resolve these concerns?

2. In your state, where is the law regulating the practice of law by nonlawyers?

3. In one sentence, what is the practice of law?

4. What are the three most commonly used categories of the practice of law?

5. Are books about resolution of legal matters UPL? How about kits such as *Do Your Own Divorce?* What are some reasons for allowing books and kits? What are some arguments against them?

6. What are three activities that people commonly confuse with UPL? Activities that are not UPL but many people think they are?

7. Can disbarred or suspended lawyers practice law in your state? Do you think they should or should not be able to? Why or why not?

8. How is the public harmed by UPL?

9. Name three exceptions to UPL rules.

10. Name three administrative agencies that allow nonlawyers representation.

11. What is the special UPL problem faced by corporations?

12. What are the three ways that lawyers inadvertently aid nonlawyers in the unauthorized practice of law.

13. What does improper or insufficient supervision have to do with UPL?

14. What does improper delegation have to do with UPL?

15. What are the penalties for UPL in your state?

---

1 ABA Opinion No. 198 (1939).

2 *State Bar of Arizona v. Arizona Land Title & Trust Co.*, 366 P.2d 1 (Ariz. 1961).

3 *Ibid.*

4 *Baron v. City of Los Angeles*, 469 P.2d 353 (Cal. 1970).

5 *New York Lawyers Association v. Dacey*, 234 N.E.2d 459 (N.Y. 1967).

6 *Le Doux v. Credit Research Corp.*, 125 Cal.Rptr. 166 (1975).

7 *Ibid.*, note 2.

8 *Id.*

9 *Id.*

10 793 P.2d 234 (Kan. 1990).

11 *Blunt v. Northern Oneida County Landfill*, 536 N.Y.S.2d 295 (1988).

12 *Florida Bar v. Golden*, 563 So.2d 81 (Fla. 1990).

13 *West Virginia State Bar, et al. v. Early*, 109 S.E.2d 420 (W.Va. 1959), and *Florida Bar v. Brumbaugh* 355 So.2d 1186 (Fla. 1978).

14 For other more recent cases in this area, see *Kentucky Bar Assn. v. Legal Alternatives, Inc.*, 792 S.W.2d 368 (1990), and *In re Bachmann*, 113 B.R.769 (1990) on typing services. Also see *In re MidAmerica Living Trust Assn.*, 927 S.W.2d 855 (Mo. 1996); *Florida Bar v. American Senior Citizens Alliance*, 1997 WL 80081 (Fla. 1997); *Oregon State Bar v. People's Paralegal Service*, 1997 WL 404081 (Or.App. 1997).

15 *U.S. v. Hardy*, 681 F.Supp. 1326 (N.D.Ill. 1988).

16 *State ex rel Oregon State Bar v. Lenske*, 584 P.2d 759 (Or. 1978), dealing with a disbarred attorney employed as a law clerk.

17 *New York County Lawyers Assn. v. Dacey*, 234 N.E.2d 459 (N.Y. 1967), in which a nonattorney wrote and published a book that advised readers on probate matters, examining whether the activity is characterized by a personal relationship between lawyer and client.

18 *Trust Mill Halted*, California Bar Journal 1, (December 1997).

19 *NAACP v. Button*, 371 U.S. 415, 83 S.Ct. 328 (1963).

20 5 USC § 555(b); *Sperry v. Florida*, 373 U.S. 379, 83 S.Ct. 1322 (1963).

21 *People v. Perez*, 594 P.2d 1 (Cal. 1979); *Argersinger v. Hamlin*, 407 U.S. 25, 92 S.Ct. 2006 (1972).

22 *Johnson v. Avery, supra*, but see *U.S. v. Stockheimer*, 385 F.Supp. 979 (W.D. Wisc. 1974), in which the district court held that defendants in a criminal action were allowed to use two disbarred attorneys to assist them in their defense under their right to self-representation. The court did not grant immunity to the two attorneys from the unauthorized practice of law.

23 L. Brickman, *Expansion of the Lawyering Process Through a New Delivery System: The Emergence and State of Legal Paraprofessionalism*, 71 Columbia L. Rev. 1153 (1971).

24 Real estate broker: *Conway-Bogue Realty Insurance Company v. Denver Bar Association*, 312 P.2d 998 (Colo. 1957); title company: *State Bar of New Mexico v. Guardian Abstract & Title Co., Inc.*, 575 P.2d 943 (1978).

25 Jerome Glaser, *Note, Unlawful Practice of Law by Trust Companies and Banks*, 32 So. Cal.R. 425 (1959).

26 *Cohn v. Thompson,* 16 P.2d 364 (Cal.App.Supp. 1932).

27 *Zelkin v. Caruso Discount Corp.,* 9 Cal.Rptr. 220 (1960).

28 *In the Matter of Easler,* 272 S.E.2d 32 (S.C. 1980).

29 310 So.2d 300 (Fla. 1975).

30 Morison, *Defining the Unauthorized Practice of Law,* 4 Nova L.J. 363 (1980).

31 149 B.R. 162 (1992).

32 594 P.2d 1 (Cal. 1979).

33 See also *In re Opinion of Justices,* 194 N.E. 313 (Mass. 1935), in which the gratuitous representation of indigents may not be the unauthorized practice of law.

34 *Johnson v. Avery,* 393 U.S. 483, 89 S.Ct. 747 (1969).

35 ABA Standing Committee on Lawyers' Responsibility for Client Protection and Center for Professional Responsibility, *Results of the 1984 Non Lawyer Practice Before Federal Administrative Agencies,* in *Unauthorized Practice in Immigration* vol. 5, 222 at n.3 (Ashbrook ed., 1991).

36 380 So.2d 412 (Fla. 1980).

37 *Sperry v. Florida,* 373 U.S. 379, 83 S.Ct. 1322 (1963). See, for example, the Indian Child Welfare Act of 1978, 25 USCA §1911(c) that allows for nonattorney representation. Since the act is federal law, the state UPL laws are preempted. See also, 9 Jour. of Para. Ed. & Prac. 1 (April 1993) for a comprehensive article on paralegal representation before the Social Security Administration.

38 For a Kentucky Bar Association opinion on the "conduit" theory, see KBA U-47, which you can find through University of Kentucky College of Law's Web site, *www.uky.edu.*

39 In *Eckles v. Atlanta Technology Group, Inc.,* 485 S.E.2d 22 (Georgia 1997), the Georgia Supreme Court held that the corporation does not have the right of self-representation. However, a Georgia appellate court allowed a corporation to be represented by a nonlawyer before the county board of equalization in *Grand Partners Joint Venture I v. Realtax Resource, Inc.,* 1997 Ga.App. Lexis 392 (1997).

40 *Travelers Ins. Co. v. Roof Doctor, Inc.,* 481 S.E.2d 451 (S.C.App. 1997) See also *Albion River Watershed Protection Assn. v. Dept. of Forestry,* 24 Cal.Rptr.2d 341 (1993), holding that unincorporated associations must be represented by a person licensed to practice law.

41 This does not include programs like profit sharing or 401K plans.

42 See *Plumlee v. Paddock,* 832 S.W.2d 757 (Tex. 1992), where the attorney paid an ambulance company a set fee plus a percentage of attorneys' fees for personal injury case referrals. The court found that the contract was an illegal business relationship as to both parties and refused to enforce the agreement.

43 *Bluestein v. State Bar of California,* 529 P.2d 699 (Cal. 1974).

44 D.C. Rule 5.4: A lawyer may practice law in a partnership or other form of organization in which a financial interest is held or managerial authority is exercised by an individual nonlawyer who performs professional services which assist the organization in providing legal services to clients, but only if:

  1. the partnership or organization has as its sole purpose providing legal services to clients;

  2. all persons have such managerial authority or holding a financial interest undertake to abide by these Rules of Professional Conduct;

  3. the lawyers who have a financial interest or managerial authority in the partnership or organization undertake to be responsible for the nonlawyer participants to the same extent as if nonlawyers participants were lawyers under Rule 5.1;

  4. the foregoing conditions are set forth in writing.

45 *Floyd v. Nangle,* 26 Eng.Rep. 1127 (Ch. 1747).

46 *In re McGuinness,* 74 N.Y.S. 1054 (1902).

47 754 P.2d 842 (N.W. 1988).

48 Ethical Consideration 3-6 sums up proper delegation:

    A lawyer often delegates tasks to clerks, secretaries, and other laypersons. Such delegation is proper if the lawyer maintains a direct relationship with his client, supervises the delegated work, and has complete professional responsibility for the work product. This delegation enables a lawyer to render legal service more economically and efficiently.

49 Negligence: *Biakanja v. Irving,* 320 P.2d 16 (Cal. 1958).

50 *Divine v. Watauga Hospital,* 137 F.Supp. 628 (N.C. 1956).

BE LOYAL TO EACH AND EVERY CLIENT

Every person involved in the field of law has a duty to use "independent judgment" on behalf of every client. What does that mean? "Independent judgment" means that the duties you owe to other people do not influence your judgment regarding a client. Let's take an example from everyday life: your best friend. Would you represent someone who was suing your best friend? No. Why not? Because your strong feelings of friendship for your friend, and all of the duties and obligations that go along with that friendship, would interfere with your ability to represent the client to the best of your ability. This is logical. Although you might want to do a good job for your client, your feelings for your friend won't let you or, at the very least, will influence you. And your friend will probably try to stop you from representing the client because of all of the "confidential" information you have about him. So, we look at the problem of adverse interests from two directions: you doing your best for your client, and the other person protecting himself or herself from your use of confidential information.

If we set aside the best friend example, we see that professional judgment is often influenced by information received from past or present clients. The essence of this Rule is that a legal professional must not compromise a client's needs and desires by outside influences or other loyalties. The legal professional owes *complete loyalty* to each client, and that loyalty should be demonstrated by (1) direct and personal contact with the client and (2) professional judgment that is not influenced by outside forces. This is a duty that we owe to each and every client: complete, unfettered loyalty. By accepting representation or even accepting an assignment on a client matter, we pledge to do our best for this client.

The ABA and other law associations and courts have repeatedly said that, in our society, effective use of nonlawyer legal professionals to aid in providing quality legal services at a reduced cost, not to "practice law" or take the place of the attorney, is <u>essential.</u> They also say that a planned, organized paralegal program within a law firm will allow paralegals to fulfill their roles and benefit the public while giving attorneys a way to remain in contact with the client and to exercise their own, independent professional judgment free from outside demands. Well, that's what they say, anyway. The reality where you work may be different. Maybe you work for extremely busy people. Maybe you work for very young or unknowledgeable lawyers. It's important for you to know the Rules regarding conflicts (duty of loyalty) that apply to lawyers for two reasons: (1) The duty of loyalty applies to you, and (2) If the lawyer you work for doesn't know the details of these Rules, you'll know, and you can use your knowledge to help the lawyer, the firm, and the client.

We divide the duty of loyalty to every client into four parts:

1. The outside interests of the legal professional that might interfere with his or her professional judgment
2. The interests of multiple clients that the legal professional is attempting to represent
3. The interests of third parties that interfere with the professional judgment of the legal professional or the relationship between legal professional and client
4. Confidential information held by the legal professional that cannot be used adversely to the former client

YOUR OUTSIDE INTERESTS

The most obvious problem in this area arises when legal professionals involve themselves in transactions with their clients. An example is when you sell your house. The couple who makes an offer on the house are your former clients, and you suggest that you can all save some money by drawing up the papers yourself. The couple, even though they no longer have an attorney/client or fiduciary relationship with you, still look at you as one who is acting on their behalf. They trust you. However, like any other seller, you are acting only in your own best interests. What's the end of the story? The sale closes and you move to another town, but the former clients become disenchanted with their purchase of the home and ask the court to set the sale aside. Who prevails? The former clients, of course. You have a higher duty to the purchasers than to people who are strangers to you, even though your earlier client relationship no longer exists.[1] You have this higher duty forever. Does this mean that you can never sell anything to or buy anything from former clients? No. You can avoid violating this Rule by advising the buyers to seek independent counsel. This would provide them with the independent judgment they need. It shields you from the appearance that you are trying to take advantage of them.

The NFPA Model Code provides the following:

EC 1-6(a) A paralegal shall act within the bounds of the law, solely for the benefit of the client, and shall be free of compromising influences and loyalties. Neither the paralegal's personal or business interest, nor those of other clients or third persons, should compromise the paralegal's professional judgment and loyalty to the client.

The ABA Model Code provides the following:

EC 5-1: The professional judgment of a lawyer should be exercised, within the bounds of the law, solely for the benefit of his client and free of compromising influences and loyalties. Neither his personal interests, the interests of other clients, nor the desires of third persons should be permitted to dilute his loyalty to his client.

Further, EC 5-2 says that legal professionals must not acquire any interest in the subject matter of employment after having accepted employment, because it would make their professional judgment less protective of their clients and their clients' interests.

Courts look at purchases of property from a client or other business relationships with a client by the client's attorney or staff members very carefully because of the inherent possibility of this sort of conflict. Historically, it has been found that the opportunity for *overreaching* in these business relationships is so significant that it warrants severe disciplinary action. Courts have held that even in instances in which an attorney has acted in good faith and with an honest intent, the mere possibility of fraudulent intent (the appearance of impropriety) is enough reason for reprimanding the attorney. That there is a possibility that you could defraud former clients or take an unfair advantage of them is enough.

Overreaching is outwitting or cheating others.

Overreaching or Fraud

We often find examples of overreaching in probate cases. The attorney who represents an estate has a duty to get the highest possible price on the sale of every estate asset. How can he do that if he wants to buy the asset for himself? If you are the purchaser, you would naturally want to pay the lowest possible price. Because of the obvious conflict between these two positions, business dealings like this must be scrutinized carefully. In a case in which an attorney had purchased an asset from an old and helpless client and misled the probate court in order to prevent disclosure of the transaction, the court found that the attorney should be disbarred. In the court's view, this activity constituted moral turpitude.[2] The same was true in a case in which the attorney made the improper sale of estate property to his wife.[3] There is no reason that the sale would be any less tainted had it been to a member of the lawyer's staff, family, or a close friend.

WHAT DO YOU THINK?

An attorney friend of yours buys and later sells a bar that he knows is in conflict with the best interests of his client. He also tells some untruths in his application for a liquor license. Has he violated his fiduciary duties in this matter? What should the penalty be? What should the penalty be if the wrongdoer is a paralegal? Is there any difference in the fiduciary duty owed by the paralegal to the client? To help you answer these questions, read *People v. Lopez,* 796 P.2d 957 (Colo. 1990).

Transaction in Good Faith

To mitigate means to lessen or minimize the severity.

There are cases where the court can find that the good intentions of the attorney may *mitigate* his or her conduct. In one such case, the attorney bought stock from a client at less than its value, but the sale was subject to the exclusive right of repurchase for the client, and the sale was made so that the client could pay off gambling debts. Although the court condemned the attorney's conduct, it held that, in this limited instance, he was acting in the best interests of the client.[4]

In another case, the attorney's initial transaction with a client was viewed by the court as being in the client's best interests. Later, however, the client asked the attorney to reconvey the property that had been conveyed to him. The attorney refused on the grounds that he was holding the property as security for his fees. The court held that it would be proper for the attorney to file a lien on the property but not to unethically retain title to it.[5]

To make sure that the transaction is in good faith, and therefore not in violation of this Rule, you need "good faith full disclosure" of all of the facts and the written consent of the parties.

WHAT DO YOU THINK?

A person who happens to be a client of your law firm owes you money. To ensure you will be paid the money, you file a lien on the client's property. The client agrees that this is the right thing to do. Have you done anything wrong? To aid you in finding an answer, review *Connor v. State Bar,* 791 P.2d 312 (Cal. 1990).

Witness

Here's another very logical application of this Rule: where you are likely to be a witness in the client's case, you have a conflict of interest and should not represent that client.

Champerty

Champerty is a term that comes to us from the common-law rule prohibiting the *assignment* or sale of a "chose in action" (a cause of action). Before there were laws preventing champerty, it was common practice for a solicitor to purchase a cause of action from an injured party. It would work like this: a poor person is injured by someone else's negligent or intentional act. The poor person does not have the ability or resources to sue that wrongdoer so simply "sells" the case to someone who has those resources. The injured person gets some small amount of money, and the purchaser has the right to sue the wrongdoer. This was finally held to be an unlawful "upholding of quarrels leading to the disturbance of society and the hindrance of common right."[6] Eventually, all contracts for the sale of a claim at law were held to be invalid. Since that overreaction, however, the law of champerty has mellowed. The problems that arise in modern law ordinarily involve attorneys who (1) buy claims, (2) accept gifts from clients, or (3) become financially involved in the litigation of clients.

> *To **assign** a cause of action means to transfer the rights to someone else.*

Speaking of a financial involvement in a client's case, isn't a contingency fee agreement something like buying a claim? In a typical personal injury case, the lawyer advances all of the litigation expenses for the client and then gets part of the winnings of the case. Isn't paying the litigation expenses "paying" for the case? The law provides that so long as the client remains ultimately responsible for repayment of these expenses, these agreements are not improper.[7] The same is true in class action suits where it is typical for the lawyers to advance litigation expenses.[8]

Unfortunately, this Rule prohibits us from helping many people who truly need help. For example, in one case the court found that advancing living expenses to a disabled client who had no means of repaying the debt other than the proceeds of his case constituted a purchase by the attorney of an interest in the litigation.[9] But a higher court later held that the unconditional obligation to repay the debt assured the court that the attorney's loan was not solicitation nor the purchase of interest in the subject matter of the claim.[10]

Repayment of costs is the key to ethical contingency fee agreements. The client agrees to pay the costs of the litigation (filing fee, deposition costs, etc.) regardless of the outcome of the litigation. If the client loses, the client must pay the lawyer back so the lawyer is not out-of-pocket on the litigation (except for the time spent). In some states, the common practice is to charge all litigation costs to the client up front so there is no question about who is paying for what.

EC 5-8 gives the ethical way to pay for the expenses of a client who otherwise would not be able to maintain the lawsuit:

> ... [T]he advancing ... of expenses of litigation by a lawyer ... [is permissible if it is] ... the only way a client can enforce his cause of action ... [and so long as] ... the ultimate responsibility for such costs and expenses ... [is] ... that of the client.

The ABA Model Rule 1.8(e) prohibits the attorney or staff members from advancing money to a client, with two exceptions.

> A lawyer shall not provide financial assistance to a client in connection with pending or contemplated litigation except that: (1) a lawyer may advance court costs and expenses of litigation, the repayment of which may be contingent on the outcome of the matter; and (2) a lawyer representing an indigent client may pay court costs and expenses of litigation on behalf of the client.

As we know, attorneys cannot escape liability for an improper act by having their employees do something that attorneys themselves may not do, so a paralegal may not give money to a client or a prospective client, no matter how great the person's need might be. It may be possible, however, for the paralegal to loan an indigent money for necessities providing that such a loan is properly documented. The paralegal should not give money or anything else of value to the client because this may give the appearance of champerty.

Friends

You work for a law firm. Your friend needs a lawyer. What could be more logical than you providing your friend with the best legal advice available (your firm) and you bringing a good client (your friend) to your workplace? How happy for everyone! Well, maybe.

If everything goes well, then it will all be fine. But if something does not go well, you may lose your friendship. For one story about friends turning against each other as a result of one friend representing another friend in a legal matter, see *www.lawyersfromhell.net*.

There is no legal precept that says that we cannot represent our friends and relatives. It just may not be a good idea from a human nature standpoint.

Publicity Rights

Another type of interest a legal professional may seek to acquire from a client is an interest in the publicity rights pertaining to the client's case. Model Rule 1.8 and EC 5-4 of the Model Code prohibit us from obtaining any media rights on the theory that this sort of financial interest may influence us to extend or complicate the litigation for publicity sake instead of ending the problem quickly, or otherwise acting in the best interests of the client.

WHAT DO YOU THINK?

Your firm's client has been convicted. While in prison, and while no longer a client of your firm, this person corresponds with you. Can you use those letters to write a book about this former client?

Model Rule 1.8(d) says:

> Prior to the conclusion of representation of a client, a lawyer shall not make or negotiate an agreement giving the lawyer literary or media rights to a portrayal or account based in substantial part on information relating to the representation.

Gifts

You should not suggest that a "gift" be made to you, nor should you accept a gift from a client. Small tokens of appreciation, such as gifts costing a few dollars during the holiday season, do not violate this Rule, but exercise of your common sense is required. The essence of this regulation is that we should not suggest to the client that we become the executor of the client's estate for a fee, nor should we suggest anything other than a normal fee or salary for legal assistance. Of course, suggesting to the client that we should inherit property under the client's will should be avoided. If a client insists on such a gift, another law firm or disinterested lawyer must draft the will.

PROBLEMS IN REPRESENTING MULTIPLE CLIENTS

Rule #2 mandates that we keep the confidences of a client. In certain situations, this is almost impossible, so we cannot be involved in the representation. The areas where this comes up are the following:

1. Seller and purchaser
2. Insured and insurer
3. Husband and wife in matrimonial proceedings
4. Debtor and creditor
5. Representing corporations and their officers, directors, and shareholders
6. Multiple defendants in criminal actions

Seller and Purchaser

If a law firm represents both the seller and the purchaser in a transaction, how can the clients be sure that each is getting the best representation possible? It would be almost like negotiating with yourself! However, it is a fundamental principle of legal ethics that a lawyer may represent adverse parties with conflicting interests *where all parties have given their consent after having full disclosure of all the facts.* It's best to look at that requirement in three separate parts: all parties—give their consent—after full disclosure—of all of the facts.

For example, if the parties have already worked out the terms of their business deal and simply need someone to document it, with full disclosure of the possible pitfalls and (written) consent, they can have one lawyer draft the documents for both of them. However, it is important to avoid not only obvious conflicts but also the possibility that a conflict will develop later, such as when a document might be subject to different interpretations.[11]

WHAT DO YOU THINK?

One attorney represents both the borrower and the lender in a loan transaction. The lenders are sophisticated businessmen. They actually hired the attorney and gave him a bonus for negotiating a loan with unsophisticated borrowers. The borrowers also retained him and paid his fees but had no knowledge of his relationship with the lenders. What should be the outcome of this case when there is a disagreement between the lenders and the borrowers later? To aid you in your discussion of possible answers, begin with *In re Greenberg,* 121 A.2d 520 (N.J. 1956).

Under certain circumstances, disclosure and consent will not be enough. For example, some courts have held that the positions of buyer and seller in real estate transactions are inherently in conflict.[12] Therefore, representation by an attorney who represented both the developers and the town concurrently was improper even though the attorney never actually engaged in any transactions between the two interests. This court suggested that, in addition to full knowledge and consent, the client must have time to reflect upon the choice and not be forced into it by the exigencies of the real estate closing. It found that the last-minute waiver obtained from the parties was only a formality and was not meaningful.[13]

In light of these cases, maybe we need to change our rule. It was *where all parties have given their consent after having full disclosure of all the facts.* If we add the words "written" and "meaningful" to the "consent" part, we may have a more complete understanding of what is required.

Insured and Insurer

If you own a car, you probably have experience with this inherent conflict: you have been involved in an auto accident. Your insurance company hires a law firm to give legal assistance to you, the insured, under a liability policy. In this instance, the law firm's client is you (the insured) not the insurance company.[14] It is possible, even probable, that your interests and the interests of the insurance company will conflict. You think the accident was not your fault. You don't want the accident on your driving record, so you want to litigate fault with the other driver. The insurance company doesn't want to incur the expense of litigation. It doesn't care who is at fault or it thinks you are at fault.

Because of this inherent conflict, the courts have held that one law firm cannot represent both insurer and the injured party, even if there is complete disclosure and consent. Courts have held that it must be an exceptional situation where the same firm may ethically represent both parties.[15] Certainly, where liability is an issue, the same firm cannot represent the interests of both the driver of the vehicle and the passenger in claims against the driver of the other vehicle.[16]

ABA Formal Opinion 96-403 Obligations of a Lawyer Representing an Insured Who Objects to a Proposed Settlement Within Policy Limits. You can find this online at *http://www.abanet.org/cpr/ethicopinions.html.*

WHAT DO YOU THINK?

Your law firm has been hired by an insurance underwriting company to prepare analyses of prospective life insurance purchasers. Your firm also does estate planning. In this situation, it is natural for members of the law firm, even unknowingly or unintentionally, to steer those estate planning customers toward investing in life insurance policies written by the other client, the insurance company. Is that a bad thing? Check out *Florida Bar v. Goodrich,* 212 So.2d 764 (Fla. 1968) to see what the Florida Bar thought about it.

Husband and Wife

Representing both husband and wife where they have the same interests is not a problem. For example, where the couple are buying a house or business together, their interests are the same and they do not need separate representation. However, in a situation where they have different interests, such as in a divorce, there is an inherent conflict. These conflicts are not always foreseeable, however. When a law firm is representing the husband and wife in a contract dispute with a third person, and the couple decide to divorce while the contract dispute is still going on, a conflict arises unexpectedly. Here the appropriate thing to do is to drop one of the couple (either the husband or the wife) as a client. It is arguable that the law firm still holds the confidential information of the one it no longer represents and so it should have to disqualify itself from the entire case. However, most courts have found that it is unfair to summarily dismiss an attorney from all representation on the case, particularly if the attorney has already put in a lot of time and effort.

WHAT DO YOU THINK?

Your firm represents Husband in a personal injury action. Later your firm represents Wife when she filed for divorce. When Wife remarries, your firm refuses to give Wife her percentage of Husband's personal injury case. Is that okay? Was there a conflict in representing Wife in the divorce? See *Columbia Bar Assn. v. Grelle,* 237 N.E.2d 298 (Ohio 1968).

Some people believe that one lawyer or one law firm can represent both husband and wife in uncontested divorces. This would help to keep the cost of the divorce down (as each party doesn't have to pay separate fees) and may well lead to more amicable dissolution of the marriage. However, typically the divorce doesn't work that way. Usually what happens is that one party has an attorney who documents the agreement that the husband and wife have worked out between themselves. Then the attorney files the divorce action on one spouse's behalf and the case is handled as a "default," meaning that the other spouse doesn't file an answer. The spouse who has not hired a lawyer can still communicate directly with the lawyer to work out any problems along the way.

Many law firms, especially firms that handle marital dissolution, post advice on their Web sites. Do a Google or Yahoo search using these words: can one attorney represent both parties in a divorce? and see what comes up. If you find a state that permits this, let me know!

Debtor and Creditor

Just like seller and purchaser, a debtor and his creditors have an inherent conflict of interest. Even when in good faith, if we represent both debtor and creditor, we represent adverse interests and violate Rule #8. Likewise, we do not want to loan money to a client because that makes us his creditor. If the client is unable to repay the loan, we owe the client our complete loyalty, but must also collect a debt from him.[17]

Representation of Corporations

The general rule is that the corporate legal professional's duty of loyalty is to the corporation, not to officers, directors, or any group of shareholders.

Model Rule 1.13 discusses the problem of the attorney representing the corporation against directors and officers, at great length:

(a) A lawyer employed or retained by an organization represents the organization acting through its duly authorized constituents.

(b) If a lawyer for an organization knows that an officer, employee or other person . . . is engaged in action, intends to act or refuses to act in a matter related to the representation that is a violation of a legal obligation to the organization, or a violation of law that reasonably might be imputed to the organization, and is likely to result in substantial injury to the organization, the lawyer shall proceed as is reasonably necessary in the best interest of the organization.

(c) In dealing with an organization's directors, officers, employees, members, shareholders or other constituents, a lawyer shall explain the identity of the client when it is apparent that the organization's interests are adverse to those of the constituents with whom the lawyer is dealing.

(**d**) A lawyer . . . may also represent any of its directors, officers, employees, members, shareholders or other constituents . . . [subject to the provisions of Rule 1.7 and] consent shall be given by an appropriate official of the organization other than the individual who is to be represented, or by the shareholders.

The cases in this area have conflicting rulings. In one instance, an attorney who had represented all the family members of a family-owned business was disqualified from representing one group of family members in an action against another.[18] In another case, two attorneys who were members of the same firm represented a family-owned corporation at the time the corporation entered into an agreement hiring a founding shareholder as president of the corporation. They had also acted as counsel for that shareholder during his years as president. The court held that it was improper for them to represent both sides in a conflict between the corporation and the former president after the president lost control of the corporation, because of the confidential information they held about him.[19]

On the other hand, where the attorneys in question said they had no confidential information that could be used by them or their client-corporation against the former president, the court held that representing the corporation against the former president was not in conflict.[20]

Just like most of this area, there are no cases dealing directly with paralegals. The best we can do to make judgment calls for the paralegal profession is to hold the profession to the identical standards as attorneys. Erring on the side of caution, we are sure to take the ethical path.

Joint Representation of Criminal Defendants

It seems obvious that you cannot work for one side of a criminal case and then for the other side because of the possibility of disclosing confidential information. Similarly, a legal professional who is part of the defense of a criminal defendant may have information that could be damaging to a co-defendant. For this reason, dual representation of defendants may be unethical if there is a possibility of breach of confidentiality.

Rule 44(c) of the Federal Rules of Criminal Procedure provides that when two or more defendants who are jointly charged and are represented by the same retained or assigned counsel, the court shall investigate the representation and advise the defendants of their right to separate counsel.

WHAT OTHERS MAY WANT

Rule #3 contains a discussion about the reasons for prohibiting lawyers and nonlawyers from being in business together, because only lawyers should make legal decisions. Where there is a possibility that someone with a financial interest in the success of a law firm (someone who is not a legal professional) has influence over decisions made about clients and cases, there is a possibility that the client, the public, will be harmed. So we say that the Rule is this: the desires of third persons should not enter into legal decisions. As is the case with most ethics Rules, there are exceptions to this Rule.

Organizations like the NAACP often hire lawyers to represent indigent people. Even though it is the organization that is paying the lawyer, the lawyer's duty is to the actual client. We saw this in the example of insurance companies and insureds, too. The U.S. Supreme Court has held that the Constitution allows for an exception to the Rule against allowing the desires of third parties to influence the lawyers' decisions in order to protect the exercise of constitutional rights. As the indigent people had no other access to justice except with the help of the NAACP, protecting their constitutional rights was a more important interest than strict adherence to this Rule.

Who's Paying the Tab?

ABA Model Rule 5.4 covers professional independence and how that may be impacted by the payment of legal fees.[21] Where someone other than the client pays the legal fee, it is possible that loyalty will be turned from the client to the source of the fee. Nothing could be more logical, but it is improper. Each and every legal professional owes complete loyalty to each and every client regardless of the source of the fee.[22]

RULE #2, THE DUTY TO PRESERVE CONFIDENCES, CREATES CONFLICTS OF INTEREST

Our obligation to preserve client confidences continues after the termination of employment.[23] Informal Opinion of the ABA 1293 (1974) states that an attorney is obliged to preserve the confidences and secrets of a client indefinitely, even after the client's death. This means that we cannot represent anyone adverse to our former client at any time in the future, even after we change jobs, even after the client dies.

Here's how it comes up: A man was employed by defendant's counsel as a law clerk and later as an associate for 3 years. He later became a partner in the firm that represented the plaintiff. Think about it: Hasn't he taken all of the defendant's confidential information with him? Couldn't he use that information to hurt his former client? His former law firm filed a motion to disqualify him from the case on the basis of conflict of interest. The court denied the motion. The issue made it into the reported cases because his earlier employer appealed. The appellate court affirmed and discussed the problems of young associates who are employed by large law firms. It acknowledged that it is common practice for young people to change jobs, and that in the course of employment they have access to confidential information of the firm's clients. The court determined it "absurd," however, to assume that every associate of a large firm would have access to every client file and all confidential information. The court held that if the prior representation was "substantially related" to the present representation, the attorney should be disqualified. A "peripheral" prior representation, on the other hand, would not be a sufficient basis for disqualification.[24]

Where's the line between "substantial" and "peripheral"? In most jurisdictions, the court will not require that the two representations be identical, nor that the legal professional actually receive confidential information.[25]

ABA Model Rule 1.9 uses the "substantial relationship" test in setting standards for accepting employment with a law firm:

> A lawyer who has formerly represented a client in a matter shall not thereafter:
>
> (a) represent another person in the same or a substantially related matter in which that person's interests are materially adverse to the interests of the former client unless the former client consents after consultation; or
>
> (b) use information relating to the representation to the disadvantage of the former client except as Rule 1.6 would permit with respect to a client or when the information has become generally known.

Presumption of Conflict of Interest

A conflict of interest may be presumed.[26] Once a substantial relationship has been established, the new representation in and of itself violates the attorney's ethical duty to former clients.

Some cases say that knowledge of an organization's internal workings will be enough for a *presumption* of conflict of interest.[27] For example, if you have access to the intimate knowledge of the company's business methods, you will never be permitted to be involved in any legal action against that company. Your prior association does not have to be continuous or lengthy. Even a brief consultation is enough.[28]

What is a presumption? In everyday language, it is something that we reason is true. However, in law we use it to mean rather the opposite. A presumption is a conclusion derived from a particular set of facts based on law, rather than on probable reasoning.

Who Is Disqualified?

If confidential information has been given to an attorney, the attorney's entire firm will be disqualified on the presumption that every legal professional in the office had access to the confidential information, even if the firm is later dissolved.[29] This rule applies to every nonlawyer employee, as well.[30] There may be an exception where the law firms are very large and the employee had no actual contact with the adverse case. To hold otherwise would effectively keep many people from ever changing jobs. There is a case directly on point for paralegals. It's on the publisher's Web site: *In re Complex Asbestos Litigation,* 232 Cal.App.3d 572, 283 Cal.Rptr. 732 (1991).

Preventing Disqualification

Before 1974, lawyers were prohibited from accepting a client if any one attorney in the law firm was required to decline the employment on conflict bases. The problem with this Rule was most difficult for those attorneys who had worked for the district attorney's office. These people had worked on thousands of cases, effectively eliminating the possibility of ever finding a private firm that could hire them without a conflict problem. As a result, it became almost impossible for government agencies to recruit bright young lawyers. In response to this problem, the ABA Ethics Committee issued Formal Opinion No. 342, opining that the prohibition should not apply to the firm of a disqualified lawyer who has been screened from participation in the work and has received no compensation stemming from the conflicting case.[31]

Ethical Wall Theory

A few years later, a court ruled against the moving party in a disqualification motion, finding that the attorney with the conflict had been effectively isolated from his firm's handling of the case and that, in fact, the firm had erected a "wall" around him.[32] Arguing in favor of what used to be called the "Chinese Wall" theory, the court discussed the inherent unfairness of turning one attorney who had worked for a governmental agency (in this case, the FHA) into a "Typhoid Mary." The purpose of the wall was to cut off communication from the "tainted" legal professional to the rest of the firm.

Ethical walls have not been accepted by all states in all circumstances. Courts in Alabama, Arizona, California, Florida, Kansas, Nebraska, New York, and Texas have expressly disallowed the use of ethical walls at some time or another;[33] in other states it is reserved for former government employees. If you are considering changing jobs, you should research your state's law on ethical walls. A good place to start is in your state's digest.

For information on how to build a successful wall, see the "How to" section on the publisher's Web site. To be of any use at all, the wall should be erected as soon as the conflict employee joins the firm. If there is any delay, it may be presumed that the conflict employee has divulged all of the former client's secrets and the firm will probably be disqualified.

But consider this: an earlier discussion teaches that all client confidences must remain confidential forever. If this is true, how can the court presume that the legal professional has divulged all of the former client's secrets to members of the legal professional's new employer law firm?

Waiver of Conflict by Client

As these Rules exist to protect the former client, the former client ought to have the right to sign a document that "waives" the conflict. Oddly enough, courts have held otherwise arguing that because the protection exists for the client, and the attorney holds an almost paternalistic position with the client, the waiver can never be made effectively.[34] Other courts have held that when written consent is given by all of the parties after full disclosure, the conflicting representation will be permitted.[35]

In today's society, and depending upon the complexity of the case and the sophistication of the client, a written waiver is still a very good alternative to the ethical wall. Remember that the waiver must be obtained from the former client whose confidences and secrets you hold. The waiver is your further written promise not to disclose those confidences and secrets or to ever use them to the client's detriment, and the client's written acknowledgement of his trust in your promise. Remember, also, as the *In re Asbestos* case illustrates, the waiver must be in writing and signed by a person with the right to do so: either the former client or the former client's representative.

Appropriate Action and Possible Penalties

In determining whether a conflict of interest exists between two clients, any doubts should be resolved by giving the client all of the facts, explaining the concerns, and allowing the client an opportunity either to consent to continued representation or to seek new counsel.[36]

After determining that there may be a conflict of interest, ordinarily there are two choices at hand:

1. Inform all of the parties of the presence of a potential conflict; bring the potential problem to the attention of the attorney in charge. If possible, get an informed, meaningful, express written waiver from the other side.

2. Withdraw from employment, or decline the employment. The conflict-employee should still make complete disclosure to prevent a possible future problem. Hiding a conflict is never a good idea.

Once the firm has been tainted by the employment of an attorney or a nonattorney with a conflict of interest, firing that individual will not help the law firm. Just as it will be presumed that individuals held client confidences during their prior employment, it will be presumed that those confidences were disclosed to others during their new employment. This is why many firms exchange a "client list" with employees directly after having made them an employment offer and they have accepted. If, after examining one another's client list, either the firm or the new hire determines that there may be a conflict problem, the offer or acceptance may be withdrawn.

Law firms that are, either intentionally or inadvertently, involved in a conflict problem may be disqualified by the court, subject to disciplinary proceedings,[37] or lose their fee.[38] The court may reverse the decision[39] or issue an injunction enjoining the communication and use of confidential information.[40] The firm may also be subject to a legal malpractice suit either by the client who was damaged or by the state bar.[41] Paralegals and other nonlawyers, of course, will not be subject to all of these disciplinary actions. Their employers, however, may be subject to them by means of the *respondeat superior* theory if their employee-paralegal has the conflict of interest. Timely recognition of conflicts and complete disclosure are crucial in this area.

This would be a good time to check out "How to Create a Conflict Check System" on the publisher's Web site.

RULE #8 WRAP-UP

Whew! This is a long Rule with lots of parts! The thrust of the Rule is complete and undivided loyalty is a duty that we each owe to each and every client. Because we owe the duty of loyalty, we have to keep things that conflict with that loyalty out of our way. Loyalty issues arise due to our outside interests such as our desire to benefit ourselves at the expense of the client. They arise when we are involved in the representation of multiple clients who have inherent conflicts of interest. They arise when someone other than the client is paying the legal fees. And they arise because we hold confidential information. Sometimes we can just avoid these conflicts by choosing clients carefully and avoiding conflicting interests. If we cannot avoid the conflict, we need to do these things:

1. Make "good faith full disclosure" of all of the facts.
2. Explain the potential conflict problems.
3. Advise the client to get legal advice from someone else.
4. Give the client time to reflect.
5. Then, get the written consent of all parties.

RULE #8 REVIEW QUESTIONS

1. What is "independent judgment"? How might your judgment be compromised?

2. What is your duty of loyalty? How do we demonstrate complete loyalty to the client?

3. Your duty of loyalty is divided into 4 parts. What are they?

4. What are some "outside interests" you have that could potentially compromise your independent judgment?

5. Name 4 instances where representation of multiple clients can lead to a division of loyalty.

6. If someone other than "the client" is paying the legal fees, to whom is your duty of loyalty owed. Why is that?

7. If you have the confidential information of Client A and now are chosen for an assignment that is contrary to A's interests, what can you do? List your options in order of the steps you might take.

8. If you have an irreconcilable conflict of interest regarding A, what might happen to your representation?

9. If a partner in your firm has an irreconcilable conflict of interest regarding A, are the consequences going to be different?

10. If it turns out that the partner must be disqualified, who else will likely be disqualified? Why?

---

1 *Miller v. Sears,* 636 P.2d 1183 (Alaska 1991).
2 *Eschwig v. State Bar,* 459 P.2d 904 (Cal. 1969).
3 *State v. Hartman,* 1194 N.W.2d 653 (Wisc. 1972).
4 *People ex rel. Kent v. Denious,* 196 P.2d 257 (Colo. 1948).
5 *In re May,* 538 P.2d 787 (Idaho 1975).
6 14 AmJur2d, Champerty and Maintenance 2.
7 *Brown & Huseby, Inc. v. Chrietzberg,* 248 S.E.2d 631 (Ga. 1978).
8 *Brame v. Ray Bilis Finance Corp.,* 85 F.R.D. 568 (N.D.N.Y. 1979).
9 *Mahoning County Bar Assn. v. Ruffalo,* 199 N.E.2d 396, *cert. den.,* 379 U.S. 931, 85 S.Ct. 328 (1964).
10 *In re Ruffalo,* 249 F.Supp. 432 (D.C.Ohio 1965).
11 *In Re Camp,* 194 A.2d 236 (N.J. 1963).
12 *In Matter of Dolan,* 384 A.2d 1076 (N.J. 1978).
13 *In re A and B* appears to be in conflict with *Matter of Dolan.* The *Dolan* court distinguished the cases on their facts, however, by pointing out that it would demand strict adherence to the rule it set forth in *In re A and B.* "A municipal attorney's public obligations are such that he must take particular pains to avoid the shadow of suspicion that inevitably is cast when he begins to entangle himself in a representative capacity in the legal affairs of a developer operating within the municipality" (at 1079).

14 *Gibbs v. Lappies,* 828 F.Supp. 6 (D.N.H. 1993).
15 *Kelly v. Greason,* 244 N.E.2d 456 (N.Y. 1968).
16 *In re Shaw,* 443 A.2d 670 (N.Y. 1982).
17 Where the good intentions and generosity of an attorney compelled the attorney to loan personal funds and the funds of family and friends to try to solve the financial problems of a client, the attorney was held to be representing the conflicting interests of both debtor and creditor. When the client was unable to repay the loans, the attorney became a creditor of the client, as well as the representative for the family and friends who had also loaned money to the client. In continuing also to represent the client, the attorney was representing the conflicting interests of himself or herself and

the other creditors as well as of the borrower (*Matter of Levinsohn*, 367 A.2d 431 [N.J. 1976]).

18 *Brennan's Inc. v. Brennan's Restaurants, Inc.*, 590 F.2d 168 (5th Cir. 1979).

19 *In re Banks and Thompson*, 584 P.2d 284 (Or. 1978).

20 *Universal Athletic Sales Co. v. American Gym, Recreational and Athletic Equipment Corp.*, 357 F.Supp. 905 (W.D.Pa. 1973).

21 The bulk of this Rule is substantially similar to DR 3-102, 3-103, and 5-107.

22 Review NFPA Model Code 1.6 and its ethical considerations on this topic.

23 Model Rule 1.6, Comment 21, and Ethical Consideration 4-6.

24 *Silver Chrysler Plymouth v. Chrysler Motor Corp.*, 518 F.2d 751 (2d Cir. 1975).

25 *Trone v. Smith*, 621 F.2d 994 (9th Cir. 1980).

26 *Cannon v. U.S. Acoustics Corp.*, 398 F.Supp. 209 (N.D.Ill. 1975).

27 *Brown v. Miller*, 286 F. 994 (D.C.Cir. 1923).

28 *In re Car Rental Antitrust Litigation*, 470 F.Supp. 495 (N.D.Cal. 1979).

29 *In re Corrugated Container Antitrust Litigation*, 659 F.2d 1341 (5th Cir. 1981).

30 See *In re Complex Asbestos Litigation*, 232 Cal.App.3d 572, 283 Cal.Rptr. 732 (1991).

31 See also Model Rule 1.11.

32 *In Kesselhaut v. United States*, 555 F.2d 791 (Ct.Cl. 1977).

33 *www.hofstra.edu/Academics/Law/law_lawrev_hamilton.cfm*

34 *In re Boone*, 83 F. 944 (N.D.Cal. 1897).

35 *Kagel v. First Commonwealth Co., Inc.*, 534 F.2d 194 (9th Cir. 1976).

36 ABA Model Rule 1.7(a); *Comm. on Legal Ethics v. Frame*, 433 S.E.2d. 579 (W. Va. 1993).

37 *U.S. v. Costen*, 38 F.24 (C.C.D. Colo. 1889).

38 *Gesellschaft Fur Dratlose Telgraphie MBH v. Brown*, 78 F.2d 410 (D.C. Cir.), *cert. denied*, 296 U.S. 618, 56 S. Ct. 139 (1935).

39 *U.S. v. Bishop*, 90 F.2d 65 (6th Cir. 1937).

40 *U.S. v. Mahoney*, 27 F.Supp. 463 (N.D. Cal. 1939).

41 *Lysick v. Walcom*, 258 Cal.App.2d 136, 65 Cal.Rptr. 406 (1968).

WORK TO IMPROVE THE LEGAL SYSTEM

The legal system, like all other systems, is not perfect. It could be made better. Each legal professional has a duty to assist in improving the legal system. Many lawyers are of the opinion that paralegals can't do much to improve the legal system, but there are others who disagree. This chapter will point out some places where you, as a paralegal, can get involved and make the system better for the paralegal profession as well as the public at large.

The late Professor Roscoe Barrow not only taught the law to his students but gave them a value system as well. He taught that the true ethics in the legal profession were not written by the legislature or the bar associations, "but were founded on the notion that the weak and unprotected people are worthy of as much effort as the powerful." The "Barrow approach" to the law was made tearfully clear to all who ever attended Professor Barrow's annual "Peevyhouse lecture."

Peevyhouse v. Garland Coal and Mining Company[1] is a case involving a dispute as to the proper measure of damages where there has been a failure to complete a contract: diminution-in-value or cost-to-complete. The picture drawn in the case is that of simple landowners who had been outmaneuvered by the oil company's corporate attorneys. The landowners (Mr. and Mrs. Peevyhouse—so we have to imagine this elderly couple on the porch of their small home in the middle of acres of beautiful open space) are convinced by the mining company lawyers that the mining company has big machines that will "roll back" the top layer of the land. Then the big mining machines will extract the coal from under the land. Then the top layer of the land will simply be rolled back into place, and all will be just as it was before. As the story goes, the Peevyhouse couple agree to the contract. The mining company comes in, rolls back the land, takes the ore from the earth, and then goes away. Wait a minute! You said you would put the land back the way it was! Too much trouble, the crafty lawyers now protest. The Peevyhouses take their case to court, but the court agrees with the evil lawyers: the value of the land is so small and the cost of replacing the land is so great that the cost to fix the land overwhelms the value of the land as it originally was . . . so, no, the mining company doesn't have to honor its word. The word of the lawyers meant nothing. The injustice of the court's ruling is clear after even a cursory reading of the case.

Annually, professors and students from all over the San Francisco Bay Area would attend Professor Barrow's lecture, many of them year after year. At the close of the lecture, Professor Barrow would inevitably single out a student sitting in the front row of the lecture hall. Barrow would point a menacing finger at him and say "Someday you, yes, you like Michelangelo, will take hammer and chisel in hand and go to that rough marble and carve a law which will accommodate our need for fossil fuel-energy and the eternal need of mankind for the land. Yes, through your creativity, to some future class, I will be able to say that the law is for Peevyhouses."[2] It was an admonition not soon to be forgotten.[3] We can learn from Professor Barrow's lecture that lawyers are evil, that they don't keep their word, or we can learn that the law itself is often unjust. You get to choose.

ASSIST IN CHANGING THE LAW

Changes in human affairs over time will necessitate changes in the law. ABA Model Rules 6.3 and 6.4 encourage the legal professional to be active in law reform and legal services organizations that are part of our changing world. The participation of legal professionals will work for the better of the legal system.[4] An example of this can be found in the history of *Molien v. Kaiser Foundation Hospitals.*[5] In the mid-1970s, Valerie Molien went to Kaiser Hospital for a routine physical examination. The examining physician diagnosed Valerie as having infectious syphilis and advised her to tell her family members about it because they might be infected as well. Valerie's husband underwent the testing, as did other members of her family and, when none of them was determined to have syphilis, family members began to fight. Husband and wife became suspicious of one another and finally divorced. All of the family members suffered severe emotional distress, but Valerie's husband, Steve, was the most severely affected. Eventually it was discovered that the doctor's original diagnosis had been in error. Valerie had never had syphilis.

At that time, California had no cause of action for "negligent infliction of emotional distress." *Dillon v. Legg*[6] was the nearest precedent, a case in which a mother alleged severe emotional distress after having witnessed a car run over her child. In *Dillon,* however, the California Supreme Court relied heavily on the fact that the mother witnessed the accident and suffered actual physical harm. It was questionable whether the California court would stretch the *Dillon* rule to allow Steve some compensation against Kaiser because he had not actually "witnessed" harm to Valerie.

The trial court in *Molien* sustained demurrers to the causes of action, stating that negligent infliction of emotional distress is not actionable in California where the plaintiff had not actually witnessed the harm to the loved one. On review, however, the California Supreme Court held that modern times demanded that a cause of action may be stated for the negligent infliction of emotional distress and further held that the unqualified requirement of physical harm is no longer justified. The attorney for plaintiff Molien had carved new law in California and championed a good cause for his client.[7] The law should and does change.

> To sustain a demurrer has the effect of throwing the case out of court.

WHAT DO YOU THINK?

In *In re Interest on Trust Accounts,* 356 So.2d 799 (Fla. 1978), a group of attorneys in conjunction with the Florida Bar petitioned the Supreme Court of Florida to amend regulations with regard to client trust accounts to allow attorneys to place client monies in interest-bearing accounts. The court's primary concern was that the monies be readily available for proper disbursement to clients and, secondarily, that the interest collected on such accounts be used for a community purpose, rather than a selfish purpose of the attorney. In approving the proposal and modifying the state's regulations in that area, the court praised the attorneys who initiated the action for upholding their affirmative duties under EC 8-15. Did these lawyers do a good thing? Is it more important to do a good thing for your client or a good thing for the public?

Rules of law should be changed if they are not just, understandable, and responsive to the needs of society. Legal professionals should encourage the repeal of outdated laws and work for the simplification of laws and legal documentation. Several years ago, California had an Unfair Competition Law, Business and Professions Code Sec. 17200, which allowed private attorneys to act on behalf of the public to sue businesses that engage in price-fixing, false advertising, or other unfair business practices. One firm abused this law to sue thousands of people, seeking millions of dollars in settlements, even though the firm had no real client or plaintiff who had been harmed. California learned that the law had been badly drafted and needed to be changed. This is a good example of a time and a place where paralegals could use their special expertise to help make the law more fair.

> If you want to know more about this, go to Google or Yahoo and type in "Trevor Law Group."

Model Rule 6.4 requires that when attorneys are advocating for changes, they must identify for whom they are working: themselves, a client, or the public at large. We can work for changes in the law that will benefit a client, even when we do not believe in the changes themselves. When acting on behalf of the public, we want to be sure that the changes are truly in the public interest.

Simplify, Simplify

One of the most modern changes in the laws has been the "plain language laws." These laws require that certain contracts and other legal documents must be in language that can be read and understood by the layperson without the aid of an attorney-translator. David Mellinkoff, author of books and articles in the area of legal writing, writes, "These laws are not, in my view, a solution, but an index of frustration. As a prod to the profession, they may do some good."[8]

Mellinkoff, in his book *Legal Writing: Sense & Nonsense,*[9] sets forth his seven rules for legal writing that will be comprehensible for the attorney, the court, and the client: don't use peculiar (legalese) when laypersons' language is more clear; use precise language when it's more clear; use the rules of English composition and grammar; write clearly whenever possible; write in simple language; plan before you write; take whatever you've written and take out the unnecessary words. These rules may seem oversimplified and are certainly redundant. They make the point, however, that legal writing need not appear to the layperson to be arcane. Lawyers have kept others at bay for many centuries by speaking a language no one else could speak. Not only did a person have to attend a special school to learn the language, but that person had to earn a certificate in order to speak it in public. Recently this prohibition, while not lifted, has been diluted. Many people are learning to speak legalese; the legislature is prohibiting its use in areas where those not versed would be disadvantaged.

To write clearly and comprehensibly, arrange your topic points carefully, use the appropriate tone, stay away from sarcasm and pretentiousness, avoid long quotations, and use precedent in your own language rather than in the convoluted prose that the court may have used.

Public Pro Bono Work

It is estimated that over 80% of the need for civil legal assistance is unmet. With this in mind, the ABA, the state bar associations, and the paralegal associations have developed measures to encourage each legal professional to donate a certain amount of time to indigent clients and render legal assistance for little or no fee.

NFPA Model Code EC 1-4(b) states:

> A paralegal shall support bona fide efforts to meet the need for legal services by those unable to pay reasonable or customary fees; for example, participation in pro bono projects and volunteer work.

The ABA Model Rule 6.1 takes a definitive stand on the subject of pro bono work and comes close to making public service work an affirmative duty:

A lawyer should render public interest legal service. A lawyer may discharge this responsibility by providing professional services at no fee or a reduced fee to persons of limited means or to public service or charitable groups or organizations, by service in activities for improving the law, the legal system or the legal profession, and by financial support for organizations that provide legal services to persons of limited means.

In California, Rule 2-102 ("Legal Service Programs") simply says that the participation in pro bono and public service programs is "encouraged." Section 6210 of the California Business and Professions Code states, however, that the legislature of that state has determined a need for free legal services for indigent persons, especially underserved client groups such as the elderly, the disabled, juveniles, and non-English-speaking persons and spells out that the state bar is to collect funds for the purpose of funding such programs. In short, the California legislature has taken an active part in increasing public service legal assistance for the needy.

Many law firms have or are developing pro bono branches. Many other law firms require their partners, associates, and paralegals to do a certain minimum number of pro bono hours per year. The growing need for pro bono representation will be an area of great importance to non-lawyer legal professionals in the future because of the comparatively low cost of their use in providing legal assistance to those who may not be able to afford an attorney.

The Unsavory Client

The question of the unsavory client is one that is the topic of heated discussion in ethics classes. Model Rule 6.2 admonishes the lawyer not to "seek to avoid appointment" of representations. The Comment admits that a lawyer is not obligated to accept a client whose character or cause is repugnant; however, the "freedom to select clients is qualified" by each lawyer's duty to take pro bono cases. The lawyer's obligation to do pro bono work is fulfilled by accepting "a fair share" of "unpopular" matters or clients.

Ethical Consideration 2-26 states that attorneys are under no obligation to represent every person, but the attorney should not "lightly decline proffered employment." This ethical consideration and EC 2-28

Law Firm Spotlight: Carlton Fields is a longtime contributor to the legal environment of Florida. It has a mandatory pro bono requirement for partners, associates, and paralegals. Take a look at its policy at *http://www.carltonfields.com* under "About Us."

encourage attorneys to take clients who may be repugnant to them or those causes that may put them in bad favor with other attorneys, members of the judiciary, or the public. By taking on these disfavored clients and causes, the attorney will be serving the administration of justice.

The questions "Must the female attorney defend the rapist simply because he wants to hire her?" and "Must attorneys take a client whose cause is overly repugnant to them?" are difficult questions to answer. The ABA's Joint Conference on Professional Responsibility encourages representation of clients with unpopular causes, saying, "One of the highest services the lawyer can render to society is to appear in court on behalf of clients whose causes are in disfavor with the general public."[10] Attorneys must not accept representation of such a person, however, if their distaste for the client or cause is so great that they are unable to render adequate representation.

All of us should consider how our personal feelings about a client or a cause will affect the quality of our work. Each and every client is entitled to the very best work product and consideration regardless of our personal likes or dislikes. The duties of competency and integrity don't change for different types of cases or clients.

WHAT DO YOU THINK?

If you are assigned to work on a case that repulses you, what are some of your options? How would you approach this with the people you work for?

Report Misconduct

The "Fink Rule," discussed in Rule #1 on integrity, also works to improve the legal system by ferreting out those who are not fit or who would harm the public.

Improper Use of the Law

The practice of law is not a vehicle for carrying out personal vendettas. When a paralegal uses his or her knowledge of the law for self-interest and vilification, the paralegal ceases to be a zealous advocate and becomes an impediment to the practice of law.

In *Matter of Crumpacker,* 383 N.E.2d 36, *cert. denied, Crumpacker v. Indiana Supreme Court Disciplinary Commission,* 444 U.S. 979, 100 S.Ct. 481 (1978), the attorney in question violated almost every ethical consideration and canon in the Code. Further, he made it a habit to sue members of his law firm and people who had been his clients and to insult members of the bar and bench. The Supreme Court of Indiana disbarred him.

The integrated state bar disciplines attorneys, as we know. In some states, it is the court system that disciplines. Discipline is not always meted out in a fair or even manner. In one case about using the law for personal improper purposes, the offending attorney didn't want to pay a personal bill. When a lawsuit was filed against him, he filed repetitive motions and a malicious abuse of process action in response. The discipline: he was suspended from practice for three years. The court said: "Respondent simply avoided paying a just bill, once again using his legal skills to retaliate, harass and damage the plaintiffs. His conduct is beyond a mere violation of the Code; it is willful refusal to admit even the slightest error."[11] Is it fair to discipline this lawyer? And what about a paralegal? If you did the same thing that the lawyer did, what would happen to you?

Criticism of Judicial System

Model Rule 8.2 implies that legal professionals should strive for fairness and competence on the bench and earnestly protest the election or appointment of unsuitable people. The criticism, however, should be fair, restrained, and temperate and must not lessen the public's image of the legal system. To maintain the fair and independent administration of justice, legal professionals are also responsible for defending the judicial system when it is unjustly criticized.

As advocates for a client, legal professionals are allowed justifiable criticism of the legal system or judges.[12] They should not, however, use intemperate or undignified language. On the other hand, legal professionals, just like the other people of this country, have the First Amendment right of freedom of speech.

The judicial system may regulate the activities of attorneys more strictly than those of the average person, however. In one case, the attorney was quoted by a newspaper as having said that courts can sometimes

Law Firm Spotlight: Robins, Kaplan, Miller & Ciresi L.L.P. has offices in Atlanta, Minneapolis, Boston, Los Angeles, Naples (Florida), and Washington D.C. The firm has 250 lawyers and over 400 support staff. In 2004, RKMC received a coveted pro bono award from the Public Counsel Law Center. Two-thirds of the firm's Los Angeles office has volunteered at Public Counsel, working on several community programs to help protect access to justice. You can find this firm at *http://www.rkmc.com*.

In *Standing Committee on Discipline v. Yagman*, 95 D.J. DAR 6873 (9th Cir. 1995), even when attorney Yagman made intemperate critical remarks about a judge being "anti-Semitic," the Ninth Circuit upheld his right to speak.

In *U.S. v. Blitstein*, 626 F.2d 774, *cert. denied*, 449 U.S. 1102, 101 S.Ct. 898 (1980), a small quantity of cocaine had been found in the possession of a young actor while he was visiting Denver on his way to Los Angeles to complete the filming of a television series. On the advice of his business attorney in Los Angeles, he hired Blitstein to represent him in Denver, expecting that charges would be brought against him. Thereafter, Blitstein and his paralegal (Pease) flew to California to meet with the actor, pretended to do extraordinary investigation on his case, intimidated him with stories of what the Denver police would do to him, and coerced large sums of money from him. In fact, neither Blitstein nor Pease had contacted the police with regard to a warrant for the actor's arrest, and there was no warrant. Both Blitstein and Pease were indicted for extortion. The Tenth Circuit Court of Appeals found Blitstein guilty, but the disposition of the court against Pease is not on the record. Since Pease's acts were of a criminal nature, Blitstein was not responsible for her under the doctrine of *respondent superior.*

be "incompetent and . . . downright crooked." The court found him in violation of the ethical canons.[13] Contrast that court decision with the court's decision in *Yagman.*

ONE LAST WORD ABOUT INTEGRITY

Model Rule 8.1 says that legal professionals should be persons of integrity. The more integrity each of us brings to the profession, the better the legal system will be. Regardless of a person's expertise or extraordinary gift for the law, the person will still be held to high standards of moral and ethical conduct, as has been the case historically. (See also EC 8-7.)

SERVE IN PUBLIC OFFICES

Did you know that about 37 percent of Congress is made up of lawyers? Why do you think that is?

It is desirable for legal professionals to serve as legislators and other public officials because of their unique qualifications and knowledge of the law and high regard for the public welfare.[14] Remember, however, that we must not engage in activities that may result in conflict of interest with our law practice or employment.

Legal professionals campaigning for public offices are still bound by the Code of Professional Ethics, even though they could hold office without license.[15] Publishing statements that are in poor taste but only political rhetoric is not grounds for discipline, but publishing statements that we know to be false probably is. Whether you are pursuing a career in law, business, or politics, you will be held to the same ethical standards. We are protected by the First Amendment's guarantee of free speech so long as such speech does not constitute misconduct under the Rules that govern us. Since the state has a legitimate interest in the conduct of legal professionals, it may restrict the exercise of personal rights guaranteed by the Constitution.

RULE #9 WRAP-UP

You've heard that quote from Shakespeare: first thing, let's kill all the lawyers. This saying accurately describes how many people feel about the legal profession—and that may include you! But the truth is that many legal professionals are out there trying to make the legal world a better place. Many people, whether through advocacy, changing the law, or teaching, are trying to make the law of America safe for Peevyhouses. Rule 9 creates yet another duty for us: the duty to make the legal system better. And despite a commonly held belief, there is a lot paralegals can do. Get elected to public office! Go to work for a firm that has a pro bono division and work on cases that deserve your hard work and dedication!

RULE #9 REVIEW QUESTIONS

1. What kinds of things can paralegals do to make the law better for the Peevyhouses?
2. How did the lawyer in *Molien v. Kaiser Hospital* change the law?
3. What is pro bono legal work and how can you do it?
4. What are legal services programs? How are they funded?
5. Could you use your knowledge of law "improperly"? Give one example of what you could do. Why would it be "unethical"? What Rule would you be violating?
6. Attorney Yagman was disciplined for using his First Amendment freedom of speech. What did he say and why might some consider it a violation of his oath?
7. Why is holding a public office helping to improve the law? If you were elected to the U.S. Congress, what laws would you seek to change? How would those changes help to improve the legal system?
8. Is there a conflict of interest between holding an elected office and serving as a paralegal? Can you think of any instances where a conflict would arise?

1   382 P.2d 109 (Okl. 1960).

2   See David L. Roth, *Tribute,* Comment vol. 1, no. 2 (Spring 1978).

3   Roscoe L. Barrow was a professor at Hastings College of Law, San Francisco, until his death in 1977.

4   See also EC 8-9.

5   616 P.2d 813 (Cal. 1980).

6   441 P.2d 912 (Cal. 1968).

7   Several law review articles discuss the legal professional's duty to better the legal system through the revision of laws. See Thompforde, *Public Opinion of the Legal Profession: A Necessary Response by the Bar and the Law School,* 41 Tenn. L. Rev. 503 (1973–74); Bell, *Improvements in the Administration of Justice,* 10 Texas Tech. L. Rev. 533 (1979).

8   David Mellinkoff, *The Myth of Precision and the Law Dictionary,* 31 U.C.L.A. L. Rev. 423, 425 (1983). See also Steven Stark, *Why Lawyers Can't Write,* 97 Nev. L. Rev. 1389 (1984), one of the shortest law review articles in history.

9   West Publishing Co. (1980). Rules cited with permission.

10 *Professional Responsibility—Report of the Joint Committee,* 44 ABAJ 1159, 1216 (1958).

11 *In Matter of Gemmer* 566 N.E.2d 528 (Ind. 1991).

12 *Committee on Professional Ethics and Conduct of Iowa State Bar Assn. v. Horak,* 292 N.W.2d 129 (Iowa 1980). See also *Matter of Westfall,* 808 S.W.2d 829 (Mo. 1991) where the attorney made televised statements alleging purposefully dishonest conduct by the court of appeals judge, with reckless disregard for the truth or falsity of the statements. The court found that attorney violated Rules 8.2(a) and 8.4(a) and (d) "... the rule, then, is sensitive to the possibility of its chilling effect and will not be interpreted to silence all lawyer criticism of the judicial system" (at 836). Also see *In re Disciplinary Action against Graham,* 453 N.W.2d 313 (Minn. 1990).

13 *Matter of Lacey,* 283 N.W.2d 250 (S.D. 1979).

14 See Model Rule 1.11(c) and EC 8-8.

15 *State v. Russell,* 610 P.2d 1122, *cert. denied,* 449 U.S. 983, 101 S.Ct. 400 (1980).

DON'T EVEN THINK ABOUT IT

AVOID THE APPEARANCE OF IMPROPRIETY

This is the last chapter of this book. There is an argument to be made that it should have been the first chapter. Maybe we need to begin here: it is not unusual for new paralegal students to be the subjects of unkind remarks such as "Why do you want to work for a lawyer?" "All lawyers are crooks," and "Lawyers are worse than used car salesmen." Newspapers and magazines frequently run "exposes" on attorney malpractice and illegal behavior by attorneys and judges. Because of the frequent emphasis on "dishonesty" in the legal field, many new students wonder if there is, in fact, a code of ethics for those in the legal profession. They are often surprised to hear how carefully attorneys scrutinize their own profession. In recent years, the legal profession has put an increasing amount of emphasis on avoiding "even the appearance" of improper behavior.

Because of the growing concern of both society and the legal profession that the profession is filled with ethical problems, more emphasis is being placed on the practical aspects of legal ethics. In the 1970s the American Bar Association insisted that its accredited law schools make mandatory a class in professional responsibility. It was not until the 1980s that the ABA placed this requirement on its accredited paralegal schools. Unfortunately, however, law school professional responsibility classes, like most law classes, emphasize the theory and not the practical aspects of the law. Many attorneys who have been disciplined for acts that did not constitute criminal behavior complain that their actions were "innocent," that they had no way of knowing that their acts were unethical. The ABA Model Code's Canon 9 "avoid the appearance of impropriety" and its Ethical

Considerations and Disciplinary Rules are the bases for disciplining those attorneys who have not broken the law but have committed an act that could have been interpreted by the public as being unethical and is, therefore, a blemish on the legal profession.

Avoiding not just obvious unethical acts but also the acts that may **appear** to be unethical is the topic of this amorphous Rule. As has been shown throughout this text, even an innocent act can take on the appearance of impropriety. Often, it will not be the good intentions of the paralegal that are recognized, but the way in which those acts are interpreted by an observer. This interpretation can mean the difference between embarrassing and costly disciplinary defense and someone's good reputation.

Conflict of Interest

Probably the most prevalent use of Canon 9 in case law is in attorney/client conflict of interest problems. In one case where the Second District was feeling its way in conflict of interest and confidentiality problems, the attorney's actions were clearly a violation of DR 9.101 (b) "[a] lawyer shall not accept private employment in a matter in which he had substantial responsibility while he was a public employee," where they could not be proven to be a violation of any other specific disciplinary rules.[1] Because this Rule's thrust goes to "appearance" and not actual "impropriety," it has been argued that consent by the former client will not protect the attorney from discipline under Canon 9.

WHAT DO YOU THINK?

In *State v. Romero,* 578 N.E.2d 673 (Ill. 1991), the former deputy prosecutor's representation of a murder defendant was improper under Canon 9 because he did not obtain consent from the appropriate government agency. If the prosecutor's job is to seek justice, and the prosecutor is required to give the defense all evidence of the accused guilt and innocence, do you think a conflict of interest like this should make any difference? Isn't the point to get the defendant the best possible defense?

Exaggeration and Zeal

Feeling frisky is okay, but not very professional. In one case, the attorney in question scribbled "WRONG" in the margin of a district judge's opinion and then submitted the marked copy as an appendix to his brief to a reviewing court. The higher court found this conduct "indecorous and unprofessional."[2] Perhaps the higher court would have found this conduct amusing on another day, but the risk is too high.

To exaggerate to make a point is human nature. In the legal setting, however, it may give the appearance of impropriety. An attorney from Alaska was disciplined for saying that a claim brought against the attorney by a former client would waive "all" attorney/client privilege because, in reality, such a claim only waives the privilege to the extent necessary for the attorney to defend himself. Although this statement was made in a letter to a lawyer, who probably knew that the statement was simply an exaggeration, the court found such an exaggeration lacking in good judgment.[3]

PROTECTING THE PUBLIC TRUST

The use and distribution of cocaine and marijuana have been held to be sufficient reason to discipline an attorney under Canon 9, even though there was no proof that the commission of the crime was related to his professional capacity. The Alaska Supreme Court held that by committing a crime related to the use of drugs, Attorney Preston had dissipated the public trust in the legal profession.[4]

Appearing in court intoxicated shows disrespect for the judicial system, in spite of the court's acknowledgment of California's strong inclination toward assisting, not punishing, those with alcohol dependency problems. Lying to the judge about the consumption of alcohol, however, was found by the court to be an unforgivable aggravating factor.[5]

In another case, offering to exchange legal services for sexual favors and having an affair with a client's wife were cause for disbarment under this Rule.[6] We learned this in Rule #1—Have Integrity. It is wise to remember that close personal relationships with clients can cause conflict-of-interest problems for you at a later time.

CLIENT MONEY AND TRUST ACCOUNTS

All of the states are in agreement with respect to the handling of client money and property. The Rules state that all money given to an attorney (other than fees and advances for costs) must be held by the attorney in a bank account that is separate from the attorney's business and personal accounts. This is ordinarily called a **Client Trust Account.** We talked about this briefly under Rule #4 on fair fees.

This is how it works: Each law firm usually has one bank account where all client money is held in trust, as opposed to a different bank account for each client. The money that clients give to the law firm as security that the bills will be paid (often called a retainer) has not been earned by the law firm until the work is actually done or the hours are actually billed to and approved by the client. This money, then, still belongs to the client but is being held by the lawyer. This money is put into an account that is alternately called a Client Trust Account or the Lawyer's Trust Account. Monthly accountings must be made on those accounts, just as monthly statements are kept on personal checking and savings accounts. In many states, the interest that accrues on Client Trust Accounts is collected by the bank and given to the bar association. This money is used to fund legal services projects and pro bono organizations within the state and is typically called IOLTA money: Interest On Lawyer Trust Accounts.[7] It shouldn't be called a "Lawyer Trust Account." It should be called the Client's Trust Account. IOLTA monies are crucial to the funding of legal services projects and pro bono organizations. However, there is an argument to be made that if the client has to have a great deal of money sitting in an account somewhere that the client can't use for something else, the client should be making interest on that money. This argument was made successfully in Florida,[8] but not in Washington.[9] The U.S. Supreme Court said in 2003, that IOLTA constitutes "taking" money but the government has the right to take money for the public good.

Securities, promissory notes, stocks and bonds, and other property of the client must be labeled properly so that they are not mixed up together (commingled) with other clients' property. All of this stuff must be held in a safe place, such as an office safe or a bank. The attorney must promptly give client property and money over to the client upon request.

To comply with these trust account Rules does not appear difficult, but lack of compliance is the source of many (perhaps most) disciplinary actions. Probably because most attorneys don't care for administrative matters, labeling client property and maintaining proper accountings have become tasks popularly delegated to legal assistants, office managers, and other nonlawyers. Remember, however, the lawyer will be held responsible for any misappropriation or misuse of funds. Delegation of these clerical and accounting tasks is the right thing to do, but supervision is mandatory.

The number of cases of attorney discipline for "commingling clients' funds" with the personal or business accounts of the attorney is staggering. **Commingling** occurs whenever the client's money is intermingled with the money of the attorney so that its separate identity is lost. If client money is placed in the position of being available for use by the attorney, remember, it will also be subject to claims against the attorney. By allowing client money to be subject to the personal or business debts of the attorney, the attorney has been in breach of duty to the client.

Attorneys have been disbarred for conversion of client funds by means of a fraudulent scheme.[10] Attorneys have been suspended from practice for commingling accounts and overdrawing their Client Trust Account.[11] In one case, a client gave money to his attorney to hold for him in an escrow account. The attorney put the money in his personal bank account until the check cleared and then transferred the money, minus his attorney's fees, into his Client Trust Account. The court found him in violation of a Rule regarding the appearance of impropriety for improperly handling client money and for failing to examine his monthly bank statements.[12] Furthermore, courts will discipline attorneys for letting the trust account funds fall below the amount they were responsible for holding for their clients.[13]

Law Firm Spotlight: Arnold & Porter LLP. Washington, D.C. was the recipient of the ABA's pro bono award for 2004. A&P has committed itself to setting a national example of law firm excellence in providing pro bono legal services. In addition to averaging more than 130 pro bono hours of legal services per lawyer at the firm. A&P also established a number of innovative new pro bono programs in 2003, including criminal defense of the indigent, federal appellate advocacy, and a resource center for the D.C. Landlord Tenant Court. The firm also took on a number of new pro bono cases in a variety of areas such as discrimination against undocumented aliens, First Amendment issues, technology sharing among countries, assistance to the arts, medical services to minority communities, domestic security and human rights, and fighting HIV/AIDS discrimination.

The disciplinary authority has an excellent chance of winning any case against an attorney that deals with the Client Trust Account because (1) banks regularly report any improper use of trust money or instances where the trust balance goes below zero; and (2) there is a paper trail provided by the bank records.

WHAT DO YOU THINK?

In *McCuin v. Texas Power & Light Co.,* 714 F.2d 1264 (6th Cir. 1983), the employment of the judge's brother-in-law as local counsel for the defendant was grounds for the disqualification of counsel and disciplinary action against him. The court held that it should have been obvious to the attorney that the sole reason he was employed was so that the defendant could make a peremptory challenge to the judge who had been involved in the case. For the attorney to be a part of such a scheme was a violation of his oath and of the "appearance of impropriety" Rule. Should this attorney have known he was being used? Is being naive an offense?

If you're wondering why this is so difficult for lawyers to understand, you are not alone. The simple fact is that lawyers are not trained to be bookkeepers. There are no "office management" classes in law school. The lawyer who strikes out on his or her own has to practice law, be the billing partner, and the office manager, and the bookkeeper all during the same 24-hour day. What's one easy solution? Hire a paralegal, of course!

RELATIONSHIP WITH THE BENCH

Rule #10 is also responsible for the proposition that **legal professionals must not state or imply that they are able by improper means to influence another member of the bar or judiciary.** This means that it is improper to tell a member of the public that one has a special relationship with a judge that would influence the outcome of a case.

It is also a violation of the Rules and Codes for attorneys to accept employment that is offered to them because of their relationship with a member of the bench.

RULE #10 WRAP-UP

It is a proven fact that the public confidence in the legal profession has been "eroded" by acts that are misinterpreted by the public as being unethical acts. For that reason, it is a requirement that we keep clients informed about the progress of their matter and explain those actions we take that may be misunderstood. Rule #10, avoiding even the appearance of impropriety, also instructs legal professionals that where ethical guidance is unclear or nonexistent, they should steer their conduct in the direction that would promote the most public confidence in the profession.

The legal profession's primary task is to aid in providing quality legal assistance to the public at a reasonable cost. With this in mind, when a question arises to which there is no clear answer, take the path toward enhancing the public's confidence in the profession. In the areas where the law is clear, such as the integrity of the Client Trust Account, no excuses will be accepted.

When dealing with ethical principles . . . we cannot paint with broad strokes. The lines are fine and must be so marked. Guideposts can be established, but in the final analysis, we will all follow our own personal moral code.

RULE #10 REVIEW QUESTIONS

1. How does the concept of "protecting the public's trust" overlap with conflicts of interest?
2. What does the idea of being polite to the judge have to do with protecting the public's trust?
3. Is the phrase "appearance of impropriety" too vague? Can you define it?
4. What goes into a Client Trust Account?
5. What items that belong to the client should be kept in a safe or safe deposit box? Why?
6. Why are attorneys so often disciplined for trust account violations?
7. What can paralegals do to prevent trust account violations?
8. Do you think that most or many lawyers are dishonest? Do you think that the public has this perception? What can paralegals do to correct that image?

[1] *Armstrong v. McAlprin,* 606 F.2d 28 (2d Cir. 1979).

[2] *Allen v. Seidman,* 881 F.2d 375 (7th Cir. 1989).

[3] *Disciplinary Matter Involving Frost,* 863 P.2d 843 (Alaska 1993).

[4] *Matter of Preston,* 616 P.2d 1 (Alaska 1980).

[5] *Ridge v. State Bar,* 766 P.2d 569 (Cal. 1989).

[6] *Grievance Committee v. Broder,* 152 A. 292 (Conn. 1930), a case still cited in the eastern states.

[7] There are and have been cases contesting this practice. Some people believe that the client is entitled to the interest that his money makes while it is sitting in the attorney's trust account.

[8] *Phillips v. Washington Legal Foundation,* 524 U.S. 156, 118 S.Ct. 1925 (1998).

[9] *Brown v. Legal Foundation of Washington,* 538 U.S. 216 (2003).

[10] *People v. Margolin,* 820 P.2d 347 (Colo. 1991).

[11] *In re Grant,* 433 N.E.2d 259 (Ill. 1982). A strong dissent recommended disbarment.

[12] *In re Hines,* 482 A.2d 378 (D.C.App. 1984).

[13] *In re Feder,* 442 N.E.2d 912 (Ill. 1982). See also, *Black v. State Bar,* 368 P.2d 118 (Cal.1962); *Cutler v. State Bar,* 455 P.2d 108 (Cal. 1969); and *Vaughn v. State Bar,* 494 P.2d 1257 (Cal.1972).

INDEX

CASE INDEX